Ultimate
CATHOLIC
TRIVIA

DEDICATED TO MY SON,

Ryan Matthew Frush

♦ ♦ ♦

Ultimate! CATHOLIC TRIVIA

1001
Fun and Fascinating Facts

Scott Paul Frush

MARSHALL RAND PUBLISHING
Royal Oak, Michigan

Marshall Rand Publishing

P.O. Box 1849
Royal Oak, Michigan 48068-1849   *www.MarshallRandPublishing.com*

Printed in the United States of America

Frush, Scott Paul
    Ultimate Catholic Trivia / Scott Paul Frush

ISBN 0-9744374-4-1

Library of Congress Control Number: 2009908007

CONTENTS

ABOUT THE AUTHOR

Scott Paul Frush received a masters degree from the University of Notre Dame and a bachelors degree from Eastern Michigan University. He is assistant vice president for investments and wealth management with Huntington Bank's private financial group in Birmingham, Michigan.

Scott with wife Christina at Saint Peter's Square, Vatican City

Scott is a self-proclaimed history buff, trivia extraordinaire, and avid writer. He and his wife Christina, daughter Gabriella, and son Ryan (for whom this book is dedicated) are parish members of Saint Hugo of the Hills Catholic Church.

From 2006 to 2009, Scott served on the Saint Hugo of the Hills parish council and was a representative for the council to the Birmingham-Bloomfield-Troy Vicariate. Scott is a former Eastern Michigan University alumni association board of director and a proud member of the Knights of Columbus (Third Degree), Catholic League for Religious and Civil Rights, and the National Italian American Foundation.

Professionally, Scott has helped people safeguard and grow their investments for nearly two decades. He manages portfolios for individuals, families, and institutions and is a strong advocate of Catholic values investing. Scott was named the 2007 recipient of *CFA Magazine's* "MOST INVESTOR ORIENTED" award, which recognizes one CFA Institute member who has made outstanding contributions to investor education.

Scott is the author of seven other books—two on trivia and five on investments. Scott has been quoted in and his work noted in dozens of print, online, and radio media outlets across the United States and abroad.

CONTACT INFORMATION

Scott Paul Frush
P.O. Box 1849
Royal Oak, MI 48068-1849

Scott@Frush.com

i

Ultimate Republican Trivia
Publication Date: August 8, 2008

Publisher: Marshal Rand Publishing

Pages: 142

Commodities Demystified
Publication Date: July 31, 2008

Publisher: McGraw-Hill

Pages: 304

Hedge Funds Demystified
Publication Date: September 17, 2007

Publisher: McGraw-Hill

▶ Named "Our Editor's Pick" by *Standard & Poor's Financial Communications*, October 2007

Understanding Hedge Funds
Publication Date: December 22, 2006

Publisher: McGraw-Hill

▶ Named "Pick of the Week" by *Notre Dame Magazine*, Spring 2007

Ultimate Italian Trivia
Publication Date: October 9, 2006

Publisher: Marshall Rand Publishing

▶ Financially sponsored by the National Italian American Foundation (NIAF)

Understanding Asset Allocation
Publication Date: September 25, 2006

Publisher: McGraw-Hill

Pages: 208

Optimal Investing
Publication Date: April 1, 2004

Publisher: Marshall Rand Publishing

▶ "Book of the Year" 2004 Finalist for Business & Economics by *ForeWord Magazine*

These books are available online at www.Amazon.com

ACKNOWLEDGEMENTS

There are some very special people I would like to thank who helped make this book possible. Many of these people are family members while some are friends I met while participating in various Catholic organizations.

A very special thank you to Fr. Ronald Richards pastor of Saint Dunstan Church for his last minute help in fact checking trivia and to Marie Doyle and Mary Young for their early support by hosting the first presentation for this book with the Saint Hugo Altar Guild.

I am most grateful to the following people who committed generous time editing anywhere from a few trivia to hundreds of trivia:

- Lorraine Meier, Brother Rice High School
- Judy DiPonio
- Howard Katz
- Jerry DiPonio
- Frank King, Saint Hugo Parish Council
- Michael Frush
- Todd Frush
- Christina Frush
- Mary Lambrix, Birmingham-Bloomfield-Troy Vicariate
- Mary Von Koss, Birmingham-Bloomfield-Troy Vicariate
- Bruce Kridler

Lastly, thank you to Kay Browne of Catholic Radio A.M. 1090 in Detroit for inviting me on her show as a guest to discuss my upcoming book.

- Scott Paul Frush

INTRODUCTION

More than 1.1 billion people proudly call themselves faithful members of the Catholic Church, the oldest and greatest institution in the world. Founded nearly 2,000 years ago, the Church has been very instrumental in shaping our global society in so many powerful and monumental ways. For those Catholics and non-Catholics alike looking to know more, such a long, varied, and rich history can sometimes seem overwhelming. Perhaps this describes you or perhaps you simply want to test your knowledge of the Church. In either case, *Ultimate Catholic Trivia* was written for you in mind. This book will help you learn about many of the most important teachings, historical events, accomplishments, holy days, pioneering leaders, holy sites, and much more.

My singular aim with *Ultimate Catholic Trivia* was to showcase the best of the Catholic Church with a focus on entertaining and educating readers. However, this book does not tell a story nor should it be considered a complete history book. There are many books of this kind readily available for those interested. Furthermore, this book does not detail any "black-eyes," whether factual or fictional, as our secular media appears more than happy to undertake that.

This is now my third book of trivia and what I initially thought was going to be my easiest to research and write. How terribly wrong was I! The history of the Church is so expansive, complex, and intertwined that I quickly discovered that sticking to my theme of 1001 trivia could be a significant challenge. I honestly could have written a book of 10,001 trivia, but that would have taken me years to complete. Including only 1001 trivia forced me to work hard to ensure that each and every trivia is fun and fascinating to most readers. I say "most" because every one of us has varied interests. Consequently, some trivia may not be interesting to you, but may be interesting to others, and vice versa. Please keep this in mind when reading this book.

For the most part, the format of *Ultimate Catholic Trivia* is fairly consistent with other trivia books. However, there is a difference between trivia books and "Did You Know" books which state a question with an answer directly following. In this book all trivia answers are grouped separately in the back in chapter nine.

No book on Catholic history can begin without a chapter on Jesus Christ and Sacred Scripture. The initial chapter in this book provides a solid introduction to many of the most important events in the life of Jesus and the apostles. However, *Ultimate Catholic Trivia* does not place a significant focus on the Old Testament nor on the non-Gospel books of the New Testament because these topics cross over to Protestant faiths and are therefore not exclusively Catholic. The subsequent eight chapters specifically emphasize all of the major periods in the history of the Church, including the ministry of the apostles, the formation of the early Church, the Middle Ages, the Renaissance, the Counter Reformation, and the modern era.

It is my sincere desire that *Ultimate Catholic Trivia* becomes both your reference guide as well as a source of fun, entertainment, and education. I've planted the seed of discovery and exploration; now I turn it over to you for your reading enjoyment. So join me for a fun and fascinating journey through all things Catholic!

- Scott Paul Frush

CHAPTER O · N · E

JESUS AND THE HOLY BIBLE

Uncovering Sacred Scripture

"Ignorance of the Scriptures is ignorance of Christ."

▶ **SAINT JEROME**

"Wherever the bishop appears there let the people be; as wherever Jesus Christ is, there is the Catholic Church."

▶ **SAINT IGNATIUS OF ANTIOCH**

4 B.C. ▶ Birth of Our Lord Jesus Christ in Bethlehem.

(1) What is the name given to the four books of the Bible that describe the life and teachings of Jesus?

(2) Who was the Roman procurator (governor) of Judea that questioned Jesus and "washed his hands" of Jesus' fate?

(3) Name the four Gospel authors.

(4) In which town was Jesus born?

(5) On which hilltop near Jerusalem was Christ crucified?

(6) On what Jewish feast day did Jesus and the apostles celebrate the Last Supper?

(7) Which Jewish high court in Jerusalem condemned Jesus to death?

(8) To what land did Mary and Joseph take the Infant Jesus to hide Him from King Herod?

(9) What is the name for the formal letters included in the New Testament directed or sent to a person or people?

(10) After the Crucifixion, which Pharisee and secret disciple of Christ asked Pontius Pilate for the body of Jesus and then placed the body in his own tomb?

(11) With what did the Roman soldiers use to hit Jesus after they had crowned Him with thorns?

(12) Who was the first apostle to perform a miracle in the name of Jesus?

(13) How many times was Jesus tempted by the devil while praying in the desert?

(14) What temporary ailment did Saint Paul suffer from for three days after his conversion?

(15) Which of the four Gospels provides us with the most information about the Blessed Virgin Mary?

CHAPTER 1

JESUS AND THE HOLY BIBLE

27 A.D. ▶ Baptism of Jesus and the beginning of His ministry.

(16) Of the original twelve apostles, how many had the same name (what today we consider a first name)?

(17) According to tradition, who were Dismas and Gestas?

(18) This person was not only a Pharisee and member of the Sanhedrin, but also a secret disciple of Jesus who spoke in the defense of Jesus at the trial before the Sanhedrin. Name this person.

(19) What is the name given to the chalice used by Christ at the Last Supper?

(20) According to Sacred Scripture, what sea did Jesus walk on during the storm?

(21) Of the twenty-one epistles included in the New Testament, thirteen were written by the same person. Name this person.

(22) What event caused Jesus to weep?

(23) According to the Acts of the Apostles, this apostle was selected to replace Judas by the remaining eleven apostles who cast lots. Name this apostle.

(24) What two groups of people did Jesus chase out of the temple, the place He called the Den of Thieves?

(25) According to tradition, what is the name for the star that marked the birthplace of Jesus on the night He was born?

(26) This woman had a dream about Jesus during His trial and before the Crucifixion. Who is she?

(27) This person—on two separate occasions—anointed the feet of Jesus with costly perfumed oil and washed the feet of Jesus with her tears. Name this person.

33 A.D. ► Descent of the Holy Spirit upon the apostles and first Christians.

(28) Who were the first visitors to pay homage to the Infant Jesus?

(29) What word did Jesus use to address God the Father in prayer?

(30) What physical ailment did Jesus cure when He told the man to, "Take up your mat and walk"?

(31) Who was pressed into service to help Jesus carry the Cross?

(32) What is the name for the power of the Holy Spirit—working through human authors—to compose Sacred Scripture?

(33) For how many days did Jesus remain on earth after the Resurrection?

(34) The word "Jesus" translates to "Joshua" in Hebrew and "Yeshua" in Aramaic. What is the single meaning of each name in English?

(35) What was the crown made of that was placed on Christ's head at the Crucifixion?

CATHOLIC TOP 10

Countries with the Most Catholics

	COUNTRY	CATHOLICS
1	Brazil	147,386,000
2	Mexico	123,393,000
3	Philippines	73,605,000
4	USA	63,188,000
5	Italy	57,689,000
6	France	45,345,000
7	Spain	39,002,000
8	Colombia	38,626,000
9	Poland	34,573,000
10	Argentina	33,389,000

Compiled by: Catholic-hierarchy.org from official Vatican sources

(36) To which town did Mary and Joseph settle after returning to Galilee from Egypt upon the death of King Herod?

(37) What relationship was John the Baptist to Jesus?

(38) Although all four Gospels point to multiple women visiting the tomb of Jesus, who is the only one woman specifically named in all four Gospels?

34 A.D. ▶ Saint Stephen, a deacon, becomes the first Christian martyr.

(39) Who were the three people from the East who followed the Star of Bethlehem to the Infant Jesus bearing Him gifts?

(40) According to Sacred Scripture, how long did Christ suffer on the Cross before dying?

(41) Name the only event recorded in the Gospels about the childhood years of Jesus.

IT HAPPENED IN 545 A.D.

▶ Death of Dionysius Exiguus, the person credited with dating the birth of Christ. His work resulted in the use of B.C. and A.D. to represent periods of time.

---

(42) The Beatitudes are only found in two of the four Gospels. Name the two Gospels.

(43) Which evangelist and Gospel writer was a physician by trade?

(44) How many times did Peter deny knowing Christ?

(45) In which river was Jesus baptized? (a) Euphrates River, (b) Jordan River, (c) Nile River, (d) Tiber River

(46) Christ's commandment to turn the other cheek replaced which well-known Old Testament commandment?

(47) The four letters I.N.R.I., inscribed at the top of the Cross used to crucify Christ, represent the words "Iuesus Nazarenus Rex Iudaeorum" in Latin. What do these Latin words mean in English?

(48) What miracle did Jesus perform on the daughter of Jairus?

(49) Complete the following words of Jesus to Peter: "Thou art Peter, and upon this rock _____."

(50) According to tradition, upon which mount did the Transfiguration take place?

(51) What is the English meaning of the word "Messiah"?

(52) What is the term for the Latin translation—although not appearing in print until a thousand years later—of the Holy Bible by Saint Jerome?

(53) According to the Gospel of Luke, how many lepers did Jesus heal and how many returned to thank and praise Him?

(54) What did the Roman soldiers do to decide who would get Christ's clothing at the Crucifixion?

(55) What is the primary difference between an apostle and a disciple?

(56) Which Gospel is thought to be derived from the memoirs of Saint Peter the apostle?

(57) For what reason did Mary and Joseph travel to Bethlehem prior to the birth of Jesus?

(58) According to Jesus, what is the greatest commandment?

Pope Pius XII

(59) What is the first book to follow the four Gospels in the New Testament?

(60) Which prophet from the Old Testament foretold the Virgin Mary and her conception of Jesus?

(61) According to the Gospel of Matthew, the Beatitudes are the beginning of which sermon by Jesus?

(62) Although Jesus read the Scriptures in Hebrew, what language did Christ and the apostles most likely speak?

(63) In which garden was Jesus arrested by the Sanhedrin?

(64) These short stories, told many times by Jesus in the Bible, are based on a familiar life experience and used to teach a spiritual lesson. What is the name for these short stories?

(65) In exchange for her Dance of the Seven Veils, Salome asked for what from her step-father Herod Antipas?

(66) Where did the apostles first encounter the Risen Lord even though they did not know it?

(67) In what form did the Holy Spirit appear to the apostles at Pentecost?

(68) What is the name given to the meeting of Mary and Elizabeth when they were both pregnant?

(69) Rank the four Gospels according to the number of chapters each Gospel contains–beginning with the most.

(70) Which same three apostles were with Jesus at the agony in the garden, raising of the daughter of Jairus, and the Transfiguration?

> ## IT HAPPENED IN 1347
> ▶ The dreaded Black Death plague rages across Europe killing millions in its path from 1347 to 1350 AD. Nearly 40 percent of Catholic clergy succumb as well.

(71) What friend did Jesus bring back to life after being dead four days?

(72) Who said, "Let it be done according to your word" in response to the angel's announcement?

(73) Which two Old Testament prophets appeared with Jesus at the Transfiguration?

(74) Name the man who baptized Jesus.

(75) According to tradition, which Roman soldier pierced Christ's side to verify that He was dead?

(76) Lead by the Holy Spirit, Jesus went where after being baptized?

(77) According to tradition, Mary lived out the rest of her earthy life in the town of Ephesus. In which present-day country–then part of the Roman Empire–is Ephesus located?

(78) Which biblical event do Catholics celebrate on Palm Sunday?

(79) It is generally believed that the original text of the New Testament was written in which language?

CATHOLIC TOP 10

Cardinals by Country

	COUNTRY	CARDINALS
1	Italy	42
2	United States	16
3	Spain	10
4	France	9
5	Brazil	8
6	Poland	8
7	Germany	7
8	India	6
9	Mexico	4
10	Argentina	4

As of February 2009

(80) Name the first book of the New Testament.

(81) Complete these words from Jesus: "Follow me and I will _____."

(82) To appease the chanting crowd, what criminal was released from prison by Pontius Pilate at the trial of Jesus?

(83) During the baptism of Jesus, the Holy Spirit was present in the shape of which animal?

(84) According to Sacred Scripture, what split in two parts when Jesus died on the Cross?

(85) What is the definition of the word "bible"?

(86) According to Sacred Scripture, how many times does Jesus tell us to forgive our enemies?

(87) According to the Gospels of Luke and John, in which languages was I.N.R.I. inscribed on Christ's Cross?

(88) According to the Gospels, who was the first person to encounter the Risen Lord?

(89) This person–the treasurer of the apostles and the only apostle not a Galilean–betrayed Jesus by identifying Him with a kiss to arresting soldiers. Name him.

(90) According to the Gospel of John, where did Jesus perform his first miracle of turning water into wine?

(91) According to tradition, what event took place in the home of apostle Mark's mother?

(92) What moniker given to an apostle is associated with the words of Jesus, "Blessed are those who have not seen and yet believe"?

(93) What did Judas receive as payment for betraying Jesus?

(94) The Synoptic Gospels, derived from the Greek word "sunoptikos" meaning "seeing together" or "having a common view of," describe three of the four Gospels that share numerous similarities. Name the three Synoptic Gospels.

(95) According to tradition, what gifts did the three Magi from the East bring the Infant Jesus?

(96) Apart from the Resurrection, what is the only one miracle mentioned by all four Gospels?

(97) According to tradition, who were Balthasar, King of Ethiopia; Melchior, King of Arabia; and Casper (or sometimes referred to as Gaspar), King of Tarsus?

The Last Supper made in salt
Wieliczka Salt Mine, Poland

CHAPTER
T·W·O

SAINTS, ANGELS, AND POPES

Exploring Those that Shaped the Church

"As the family goes, so goes the nation, and so goes the whole world in which we live."

▶ POPE JOHN PAUL II

"Every evil, harm, and suffering in this life comes from the love of riches."

▶ SAINT CATHERINE OF SIENA

(98) Born in Siena, Italy, this saint was a tertiary of the Dominican Order, a scholastic theologian, and worked to bring the papacy back to Rome from Avignon. Name this woman proclaimed a "Doctor of the Church" in 1970.

(99) What are "regnal" names?

(100) The reign of a pope is commonly referred to by what name?

(101) How many archangels are recognized by the Catholic Church?

(102) What plant with three leaflets and one stem did Saint Patrick say was symbolic of the Holy Trinity?

(103) Who was the first pope from Poland and only pope of Slavic heritage?

(104) This saint established the Abbey of Monte Cassino in Italy and established the Benedictine Order in 530. Name this saint considered the "Father of Monasticism in the West."

IT HAPPENED IN 1773

▶ Following their expulsion from Portugal in 1759, from France in 1764, and from Spain in 1767, the Jesuits were suppressed by a brief from Pope Clement XIV. This crippling ban was based on erroneous information and unsubstantiated accusations.

(105) Santa Claus is the nickname for which saint?

(106) In addition to Saints Elias Nieves and Joseph, who is a patron saint of Mexico?

(107) According to tradition, which angels–typically pictured wearing crowns–move the stars and planets and ensure the cosmos remains in order?

(108) This 3rd-century saint is not only a patron saint of musicians and a patron saint of poets, but also–according to legend–the inventor of the organ. Name her.

(109) Which two popes died at Castel Gandolfo during the 20th century?

CHAPTER 2

(110) Assigned by God, this celestial spirit prays for us, protects and guides us, and offers our prayers, good works, and desires to God. What is the name for this celestial spirit?

(111) Name the three <u>biblical</u> archangels.

(112) What does the word "pope" mean in English? (a) Father, (b) Leader, (c) Believer, (d) Teacher

(113) When electing a new pope, how many times each day are ballots cast by the papal conclave?

(114) Which pope was posthumously awarded the United States Presidential Medal of Freedom in 1963?

(115) This saint founded the Jesuit Order in 1540, today the largest Catholic Order in the world. Name this saint.

(116) Born in Italy in 1181, I am a deacon that founded the Franciscan Order in 1209. Who am I?

(117) Who wrote *Love and Responsibility*, *Memory and Identity*, *Crossing the Threshold of Hope*, and *The Jeweler's Shop*?

(118) According to tradition, what is the symbolic object or sign associated with Saint Dominic?

(119) What is the birth name of Pope John Paul II?

(120) Issued by the pope, this solemn document is a written statement bearing the pope's official lead seal. What is this document called?

(121) What breed of dog is named after a saint?

(122) Are papal elections carried out by secret or open ballot?

(123) This saint and Bishop of Hippo was one of the Catholic Church's greatest theologians. Name this "Doctor of the Church" who converted—due to the prayers of his mother Saint Monica—to Christianity after many sinful years.

(124) This person, one of the two patron saints of France, saw visions of saints telling her to save France from defeat in the Hundred Years' War against England. Name this person not canonized until nearly five centuries after her death.

(125) Who was the second pope who reigned from 67 A.D. to 76 A.D.?

(126) According to tradition, Saint Anne and Saint Joachim were the parents of whom?

Future Pope John Paul II

(127) Saint Peter is frequently depicted holding two of what item?

(128) How long was the pontificate of Pope John Paul I?

(129) The second largest religious procession in the world is held annually in Catania, Sicily on February 5th. Which official memorial do Sicilians celebrate on this day?

(130) Blessing of the throats occurs on the optional memorial day of which saint? (Hint: February 3rd)

(131) What is the name for a formal letter–usually on doctrine–written by a pope to either bishops or the entire Church?

(132) In what year was future Pope John Paul II ordained a priest in Poland? (a) 1946, (b) 1949, (c) 1952, (d) 1959

(133) Born Count Vincenzo Gioacchino Raffaele Luigi Pecci, this pope reigned from 1878 to 1903 and was the oldest pope at age ninety-three. Name this pope called the "Workingman's Pope."

SAINTS, ANGELS, AND POPES

195 ▶ Pope Victor I, the first African pope, is elected.

(134) Which apostle is a patron saint of bankers and stockbrokers?

(135) According to tradition, which choir of angels is considered the angels of harmony and wisdom?

(136) Which two popes were beatified in September 2000?

(137) Which saint met the Christ Child on the beach while reflecting on the Holy Trinity?

(138) What breakfast dish, dating to the early-18th century, was named for Pope Benedict XIII?

(139) What word describes the physical remains and effects of saints that are considered worthy of veneration by the Church?

(140) Born Fernando Martins de Bulhões in Portugal, this saint and "Doctor of the Church" is traditionally depicted in artwork holding the Christ Child in his arms. Who is this saint known as the Franciscan miracle worker?

(141) Who is the patron saint of priests?

CATHOLIC TOP 10
U.S. States with the Highest Proportion of Catholics

	STATE	PERCENTAGE
1	Rhode Island	59%
2	Massachusetts	42%
3	New Jersey	41%
4	Connecticut	37%
5	New York	36%
6	Nevada	33%
7	Illinois	30%
8	Pennsylvania	29%
9	Wisconsin	29%
10	Louisiana	28%

Source: Catholic Almanac 2009

(142) As a boy, this well-known Catholic leader suffered a fractured skull—nearly killing him—after being struck by a truck. Name him.

(143) Who is the patron saint of spiritual help?

(144) Which 20th-century pope was the first pope to be canonized since the 17th century?

(145) This saint was the first recorded person to receive the stigmata in 1224 after forty days of fasting. He received the stigmata frequently during the last two years of his life before dying in 1226. Name this saint.

(146) What do Pope Marcellinus, Pope Liberius, Pope Benedict IX, Pope Gregory VI, Pope Saint Celestine V, and Pope Gregory XII share in common?

(147) According to some evidence, what honor does Pope Saint Siricius, who reigned from 384 to 399, hold?

(148) This woman, the patron saint of South America, was so beautiful that people referred to her by the name of a flower. Who is she?

(149) Nicholas Breakspear was the birth name of the only English pope. What was his regnal name?

(150) In 1937, Pope Pius XI wrote the encyclical *Divini Redemptoris*. What specifically did this encyclical condemn? (Hint: Lenin)

(151) How long was the pontificate of Pope John Paul II?

(152) Which pope wrote the famous encyclical titled *Quadragesimo Anno*, reaffirming the Church's commitment to labor?

(153) This title is given by the Church to saints and blesseds who suffered persecution and torture for their faith, but not to the point of death. Name this title.

(154) This English statesman and Lord Chancellor under King Henry VIII was beheaded–by edict of King Henry–for his opposition to King Henry's divorce. Name this person.

(155) Who are the creatures with intelligence and free will who act as messengers for God?

(156) This ring–engraved with Saint Peter fishing from a boat–was a signet used until 1842 to seal official documents signed by popes. Name this ring.

(157) This pope canonized 483 saints–more than the combined tally of his predecessors during the previous five centuries. Name him.

(158) Born in Italy in 1850, this person became an American citizen in 1909 and became the first American saint when canonized by Pope Pius XII on July 7, 1946. Name this person.

(159) This saint and apostle has a cross in the shape of an "X" as his emblem. Name him.

(160) Pope Clement II, who reigned from 1046 to 1047, is the only pope ever to be buried in which country?

(161) After Pope Saint Peter, which pope reigned the longest in Church history at thirty-one years, seven months, and twenty-three days?

(162) Who are the last three non-Italian popes and their nationalities?

(163) What honor does Blessed Kateri Tekakwitha (1656–1680) hold?

> **IT HAPPENED IN 34 A.D.**
>
> ▶ Saint Paul was converted and baptized as a Christian. After three years of solitude in the desert, he began his ministry and embarked on three major missionary journeys. Saint Paul is recognized as the Apostle to the Gentiles and was imprisoned twice in Rome and beheaded there between 64 and 67.

(164) This "Prince of Theologians" wrote over fifty works that logically and objectively–rather than through faith and revelation–defend the Church and its doctrines. His masterpiece is *Summa Theologica*, a book famous for its five logical arguments for the existence of God. Name this saint and Dominican.

(165) This person is not only one of the three patron saints of Ireland, but also considered the founding father of the Catholic Church in Ireland. Name him.

(166) In 1582, this pope corrected flaws in the older Julian calendar dating to 46–45 B.C. by advancing the calendar date ten days in order to bring the calendar in line with the natural course of the seasons–thus creating the modern (or Reformed) calendar. Name this pope.

(167) In addition to Saint Sebastian, who is the patron saint of policemen?

(168) Has there ever been a pope of Jewish heritage?

(169) Where in Italy can you find a painting of the Crucifixion that, according to tradition, spoke to Saint Thomas Aquinas?

(170) This Monastic Order has produced fifty popes, 200 cardinals, 7,000 archbishops, 15,000 bishops, and over 1,500 saints. Name this Order referred to as the "Black Monks."

(171) This apostle and saint was crucified under Roman Emperor Nero upside-down–per his request–on the cross because he did not believe that he deserved to be crucified in the same manner as Christ. Name him.

(172) Which base regnal name has been shared by popes throughout history more than any other regnal name?

(173) According to tradition, what is the symbolic object or sign associated with Saint Vincent de Paul?

(174) In addition to the Blessed Virgin Mary, which saint is depicted in artwork more than any other saint?

(175) Which pope convoked the Second Vatican Council to reflect pastoral orientation toward renewal and reform in the Church?

(176) Who is the patron saint of politicians?

(177) Popes Pius XI and Pius XII would leave the Vatican for their summer residence to avoid meeting with a certain dictator. In addition, the popes even closed the Sistine Chapel for "repairs" to keep this person from seeing the inside. Name this dictator.

(178) Born Albino Luciani, this person was the first pope to use "first" in his regnal name. Name this pope nicknamed the "smiling pope."

(179) Which saint and Carmelite nun is known as the "Little Flower"?

(180) This pope was both the first pope ever to visit a synagogue and the first pope ever to visit a mosque. Name him.

(181) Who is the patron saint of the United States?

(182) Saint Gregory the Great and Saint John Baptist de la Salle are together the patron saints of whom?

Saint Frances Xavier Cabrini

(183) Who is the patron saint of grandfathers?

(184) Who is the patron saint of both married couples and carpenters?

(185) How many popes resided in Avignon?

(186) What is unique about the name Pope Marcellus II who reigned in A.D. 1555?

(187) This priest became the first victim of the Nazi consecration camps to be canonized when he volunteered to take the place of a father of several children who was scheduled for execution at Auschwitz during World War II. Name this saint who is honored with a statue in Krakow, Poland.

(188) Which pope had the shortest pontificate at only thirteen days?

(189) A declaration by the pope that a deceased person is raised to the full honors of the altar (i.e. saint) after having been beatified is referred to by what name?

(190) As a new pope, which pope scheduled his introductory ceremony around a major soccer match?

(191) Where was Saint Peter crucified and buried?

CATHOLIC TOP 10

Popes with the Longest Reigns

	POPE	PONTIFICATE
1	Pius IX	31 years, 7 months, and 23 days
2	John Paul II	26 years, 5 months, and 18 days
3	Leo XIII	25 years, 5 months, and 1 day
4	Pius VI	24 years, 6 months, and 15 days
5	Adrian I	23 years, 10 months, and 25 days
6	Pius VII	23 years, 5 months, and 7 days
7	Alexander III	21 years, 11 months, and 24 days
8	St. Sylvester I	21 years, 11 months, and 1 day
9	St. Leo I	21 years, 1 month, and 13 days
10	Urban VIII	20 years, 11 months, and 24 days

(192) Which former two popes does the name "Pope John Paul I" honor?

(193) Who is the patron saint of Catholic schools?

(194) What is done with the pope's ring upon his death to symbolize the end of that pope's authority?

(195) Michael the Archangel is traditionally shown holding what item?

(196) In which century did popes begin changing–with few exceptions– their names upon becoming pope?

(197) This saint is a "Doctor of the Church" and the patron saint of librarians. Name this saint whose memorial is celebrated on September 30th.

(198) Which Italian saint started the Christmas tradition–first begun for the midnight Christmas Mass in 1223–of restaging the nativity scene to commemorate the birth of Jesus?

(199) The first canonization in modern Church history to take place outside Rome occurred on May 6, 1984 by Pope John Paul II. In which country did this canonization occur?

(200) Which saint is symbolized by a flaming torch?

(201) What personal item did Pope John Paul II give to the Shrine of Our Lady of Fátima church?

(202) This saint, called the Navigator or Voyager, was one of the Twelve Apostles of Ireland and, according to legend, crossed the Irish Sea in a leather boat. Name this Irishman.

(203) Who is the patron saint of expectant mothers?

(204) In what year was Pope John Paul II elected by the papal conclave (an assembly of cardinals)?

(205) Saint Benedict, founder of the Benedictine Order, and his twin sister are buried together at the Abbey of Monte Cassino. Name the twin sister and saint.

(206) What is the meaning behind the name Saint Michael the Archangel?

Ultimate Catholic Trivia

343-44 ► Popes—by bishop appeal–given highest authority in the Church.

(207) On which date do Catholics celebrate the optional memorial of Saint Patrick with some marking the day by wearing green?

Pope Pius X

(208) Which pope canonized the second most saints in Church history behind Pope John Paul II?

(209) According to tradition, what is the symbolic object or sign associated with Saint Matthew?

(210) Which play, made into a television show starring Burt Lancaster, was written by Pope John Paul II in 1960?

(211) According to tradition, what is the symbolic object or sign associated with Saint Jerome?

(212) Who is the patron saint of travelers and the saint to whom Catholics pray to for help in finding lost items?

(213) Born Angelo Giuseppe Roncalli, this pope served in the Italian Army as a chaplain and as a stretcher-bearer in the medical corps during World War I. What is his papal name?

CHAPTER
T·H·R·E·E

VATICAN, SHRINES, AND CHURCHES

Investigating Holy Sites and Pilgrimage Destinations

"Every guest who comes to the monastery shall be received as if he were Christ himself."

▶ **SAINT BENEDICT**

"I am the servant of the servants of God."

▶ **POPE SAINT GREGORY THE GREAT**

23

(214) In which palace did popes reside–prior to Avignon and the Apostolic Palace–for the one thousand year period between the 4th and 14th centuries?

(215) Which Italian Renaissance artisan was commissioned to paint the ceiling and wall behind the altar in the Sistine Chapel?

(216) The "Holy See" refers to what?

(217) The principal church of a diocese/archdiocese and official church of a bishop/archbishop is referred to by what name?

(218) How many popes have there been ending with Pope Benedict XVI?

(219) What was the Vatican's *Index Librorum Prohibitorum*?

(220) Established in 1506 by Pope Julius II, this group of men is charged with protecting the pope. Name this group.

(221) Located in Mexico, this basilica is the second most visited Catholic shrine in the world. Name this basilica.

IT HAPPENED IN 1097-1099

▶ The first Crusades to the Holy Land were undertaken with the initial goal of recovering the territory and its holy places, thus permitting free access to Christians.

---

(222) What is the title for a person who sat on the papal throne but whose election was declared uncanonical some time later by the Vatican?

(223) What minimal salary do popes receive from the Vatican for their service?

(224) What two colors comprise the background of the papal flag?

(225) True/False: The Cathedral of Notre-Dame of Paris is owned by the French government and not the Catholic Church.

(226) What is another name for a monastery?

---

(227) Who was the very first pope to select a double regnal name?

(228) With a total area of 227,070 square feet, this structure can accommodate 60,000 people in its expansive area making it the largest church in all of Christendom. Name this structure.

(229) Name the teaching office or authority of the Roman Catholic Church.

(230) This Vatican tribunal primarily, but not exclusively, addresses legal questions regarding Catholic marriage, specifically annulment cases. Name this court.

(231) How many miles of book shelves does the Vatican Library use to hold its over one million books?

(232) How many altars are located within Saint Peter's Basilica?

(233) What is unique about the ATM (Automated Teller Machine) operated by the Institute for Works of Religion, commonly known as the Vatican Bank?

(234) This fresco, the largest fresco produced during the Renaissance, was painted by Michelangelo and covers the entire wall behind the altar in the Sistine Chapel. Name this fresco that took years to complete.

(235) What physically denotes the border between the State of the Vatican City and Italy?

(236) What is the language used to give commands within the Swiss Guard?

(237) What is a chancery?

(238) This basilica honoring the Blessed Virgin Mary is the largest Catholic church in the United States and the eighth largest religious structure in the world. Name this basilica.

(239) According to tradition, the body of Jesus was prepared for burial on the Stone of Unction. Inside which church is this stone located today?

(240) Name the highest judicial authority (court) in the Catholic Church besides the pope himself, who is the supreme ecclesiastical judge.

CATHOLIC TOP 10

Major Countries with Highest Percentage of Catholics

	COUNTRY	PERCENTAGE
1	Italy	96.6%
2	Poland	94.3%
3	Paraguay	91.6%
4	Portugal	90.4%
5	Ecuador	89.6%
6	Argentina	89.3%
7	Venezuela	87.8%
8	Spain	87.8%
9	Peru	87.8%
10	Mexico	86.7%

Compiled by: Catholic-hierarchy.org from official Vatican sources

(241) In which country can you find the Shrine of Our Lady of Knock where an apparition of the Blessed Virgin Mary, Saint Joseph, and Saint John the apostle was witnessed by fifteen people in 1879?

(242) Transported from Jerusalem to Rome, these twenty-eight marble steps—now encased by wooden coverings—are believed to have been walked by Jesus when He met Pontius Pilate. Today, many Catholics climb these steps on their hands and knees and say a prayer after each step climbed. Name these steps.

(243) What is the highest Order within the Papal Orders of Chivalry?

(244) What is the longest amount of time in Church history the cardinals needed to elect a new pope when Pope Gregory X was elected on September 1, 1271?

(245) This well-known Gothic cathedral contains the cathedra, or official chair, of the Archbishop of Paris, France. Name this cathedral.

(246) True/False: A pope's pontificate begins at his coronation.

(247) As of July 2009, how many people are considered citizens of the State of the Vatican City?

(248) This group of clergymen advises the pope on Church matters when summoned for an ordinary consistory but has no ruling power except during a papal vacancy. Name this group.

(249) What is the present name for the former Catholic church where British monarchs are crowned?

(250) Derived from the ancient Latin word "nuntius," meaning "envoy," this person is a permanent diplomatic ambassador of the Holy See to a state or international organization. Name the title for this ambassador.

(251) How many Swiss Guards protect the pope?

(252) Which Italian inventor established and supervised Vatican Radio until his death in 1937?

(253) Due to a sequencing error made in the 10th century, the Vatican skipped which regnal name in order to correct the error?

(254) How many Swiss Guards died protecting Pope Clement VII during an attack on the Vatican by Emperor Charles V in 1527?

The Last Judgment by Michelangelo

(255) What is the official penalty for a cardinal who breaks the oath of secrecy regarding papal elections?

(256) What is the official language–apart from the Holy See–of the State of the Vatican City?

(257) Where specifically does the Vatican Obelisk stand?

(258) What majority of the papal conclave is needed to elect a new pope?

(259) In 1975, Pope Paul VI decreed that cardinals over a certain age are not eligible to vote in papal elections. What is this age limit?

(260) What is the name of the 1929 treaty–superseded by a 1985 concordat–that established the State of the Vatican City?

(261) Where at the Vatican does the pope reside?

(262) What papal document is not only less formal than a papal bull, but also concerns less serious matters than a papal bull?

(263) What language, sometimes referred to as "Church Latin," is the standard language for official Church documents and Canon Law?

(264) What is the oldest church, founded in the 6th century, located within the Vatican and said to be a place where Charlemagne worshipped?

(265) How many popes throughout history have abdicated?

(266) Which Vatican official has the privilege of announcing the results of papal elections to the waiting crowds?

(267) Which grotto in France is visited by four to six million pilgrims each year?

(268) True/False: The State of the Vatican City is one of a few countries that is not a member of the United Nations.

(269) In which year did Vatican Radio first broadcast, albeit in Morse Code?

(270) Approximately how many lay people work at the Vatican?

(271) This cathedral, built by Constantine in the 4th century, is not only the cathedral of the Bishop of Rome (thus the papal throne), but also the highest ranking church above all others in the Catholic Church–even above Saint Peter's Basilica. Name this cathedral.

(272) What is the time limit cardinals have for electing a new pope?

(273) The Church of the Multiplication in Tabgha, Israel commemorates which miracle of Jesus?

(274) Why is the left foot of the seated bronze statue of Saint Peter in Saint Peter's Basilica worn and shinny?

(275) How large is the State of the Vatican City as measured in acreage of land?

IT HAPPENED IN 1992

► The case dating to the 17th century against Italian physicist, mathematician, and astronomer Galileo Galilei is officially closed by the Vatican in favor of Galilei.

(276) Name the parish church of Vatican City.

(277) In 2007, this "Patriarch of Babylon" became the first Chaldean Catholic to be elevated to the rank of cardinal within the Catholic Church. Name him.

(278) What is the name for the bulletproof motor vehicles used by the pope during outdoor public appearances?

(279) This shrine, located at Our Lady of the Angels Monastery in a remote area of Alabama, was founded by Mother Angelica and is home to the Poor Clare Nuns of Perpetual Adoration, a cloistered Franciscan Order. Name this shrine.

(280) When Polish Cardinal Karol Wojtyla became Pope John Paul II in 1978, he became the first non-Italian pope in how many years? (a) 77, (b) 123, (c) 456, (d) 671

(281) How many popes had the regnal name John XXIII?

(282) Adopted by a Swiss family, Dhabi Bachammwas is the first non-European born Swiss Guard. Where was he born?

Basilica of the National Shrine of the Immaculate Conception

(283) What is *L'Osservatore Romano*, Latin for *The Roman Observer?*

(284) Only one Catholic Order can absolve the sins of the pope. Name this Catholic Order.

(285) Who wrote *Dialogue*, a book that describes the entire spiritual life of humans through a series of conversations between God and the soul?

(286) What must be performed by the cardinals if a pope is not elected by the papal conclave in three days?

(287) What are the three colors found in the uniform of the Swiss Guard?

(288) The Basilica of the National Shrine of Our Lady of Aparecida is considered the second largest Catholic church building in the world after Saint Peter's Basilica. In which country is this basilica located?

(289) This Vatican office—entrusted to a friar of the Order of Preachers (Dominicans)—is considered the pope's personal theologian. Name this office.

(290) This type of cross—although not commonly used today—has three straight horizontal bars, in diminishing order of length near the top, attached to one vertical bar. Name this cross.

VATICAN, SHRINES, AND CHURCHES

496 ▶ Franks become a Catholic people upon the conversion of Clovis.

(291) An assembly of Cardinals formed to elect a pope is referred to by what name?

(292) What are the titles or names for the four official steps in the canonization process?

(293) Aside from announcing that a new pope is elected, on what four fixed occasions is the ten-ton bell in the dome of Saint Peter's Basilica rung?

(294) This person, responsible for many tasks similar to those of senior level diplomats, is considered the second most important person at the Vatican after the pope himself. What is the title of this person?

(295) Established by Pope Pius X, this publication is the official gazette of the Vatican appearing about twelve times per year. Name this publication. (Hint: not the daily newspaper of course)

(296) What papal document details the life and works of a pope and testifies to his burial?

(297) What is the title for a bishop appointed to act as the representative of the pope in an area not yet designated a diocese?

(298) What is the name for the period of time between the death of a pope and the election of his successor?

(299) This former volunteer military unit of nearly 4,500 mainly unmarried Catholic men from around the world was formed to defend the Papal States against hostile forces of the Italian Risorgimento during the 19th century. Name this now-disbanded military unit.

(300) What is the name of the famous sculpture inside Saint Peter's Basilica where Jesus is lying on Mary's knees after the Crucifixion?

(301) According to one legend, this saint was beaten and beheaded on February 14, 270 for violating Roman law by secretly marrying couples. Name him.

(302) Set by Pope Paul VI in 1973, the number of cardinal electors is limited to how many?

(303) Where can you find the Bernini Colonnade?

(304) In addition to releasing smoke, what does the Vatican do—to ensure no mistakes were made with the smoke—to signal that a new pope has been elected?

(305) Where specifically would you go to visit the papal observatory?

(306) Who were the theological experts who attended the Second Vatican Council and acted in the capacity of counselors to the bishops and cardinals?

(307) What bodily relic—miraculously preserved while the rest of his body had returned to dust—from Saint Anthony is contained in a reliquary in his shrine in Padua, Italy?

IT HAPPENED IN 1545

▶ The Ecumenical Council of Trent is convened to mobilize the Counter-Reformation movement. This council, closed in 1563, issued a significant number of important decrees ranking it—along with Vatican II—as the greatest ecumenical council held in the West.

(308) How many popes are buried at Saint Peter's Basilica?

(309) Who are the administrators of the Holy See and the central governing body of the entire Catholic Church, together with the pope?

(310) How are the doors of the Sistine Chapel sealed after cardinals gather to elect a new pope?

(311) True/False: Saint Peter's Basilica is taller than the Statue of Liberty.

(312) What are the traditional weapons of the Swiss Guards?

(313) What is unique about the dimensions of the papal flag?

CHAPTER 3

(314) In July 2007, the Vatican agreed to become the first carbon-neutral state by creating a Vatican climate forest to offset carbon dioxide emissions. In which country does the Vatican plan to create and manage this forest?

(315) From whom does the Sistine Chapel take its name?

(316) What is the name for the bishop's physical seat or throne in a cathedral church?

(317) How do all Vatican Radio broadcasts begin?

(318) This three-tiered jeweled papal crown, supposedly of Byzantine and Persian origin, is a prominent symbol of the papacy first worn by Pope Clement V and ended with Pope Paul VI in 1963 when he chose the miter instead. Name this crown.

(319) About how many items does the Vatican Secret Library supposedly hold?

(320) Upon the death of a pope, who becomes head of the College of Cardinals and then directs the Conclave?

(321) True/False: Saint Peter's Basilica is not a cathedral.

(322) Which shrine dedicated to Mary features a natural spring?

(323) Of the 265 popes, only fifty-eight have been of non-Italian heritage. What two ethnic groups are tied for the second most popes with fifteen each?

(324) Built in 1573 by Pope Gregory XIII as a papal summer residence, this palace served as the official residence for popes until 1870 when Rome became the capital of the new Kingdom of Italy and the palace involuntarily became the official royal residence of the kings of Italy. Name this palace.

(325) What was originally on the ceiling of the Sistine Chapel prior to Michelangelo's fresco?

(326) To signal that a new pope was not elected, black smoke is released from the Vatican. What two items–after being bound together with needle and thread–and burnt to produce this black smoke?

(327) Although there have been 265 popes, how many pontificates (reign of a pope) have there been?

CATHOLIC TOP 10

U.S. Sponsored Theologates with Highest Enrollments

	THEOLOGATE	CANDIDATES
1	Mundelein Seminary – St. Mary of the Lake, IL	187
2	North American College, Rome	186
3	Catholic Theological Union, IL	158
4	Mount St. Mary's Seminary, MD	154
5	Immaculate Conception Seminary, NJ	123
T6	Sacred Heart School of Theology, WI	109
T6	Saint Meinrad School of Theology, IN	109
8	Oblate School of Theology, TX	107
9	St. John Vianney Theological Seminary, CO	104
10	St. Patrick's Seminary and University, CA	99

Source: Center for Applied Research in the Apostolate, Georgetown University, 2008-2009

CHAPTER IV

F·O·U·R

EVENTS, ORIGINS, AND MISCELLANEOUS

Revealing Pivotal Times in Church History

"Not a hundred people in the United States hate the Roman Catholic Church, but millions hate what they mistakenly think the Roman Catholic Church is."

▶ BISHOP FULTON J. SHEEN

"When I am at Rome, I fast on a Saturday: when I am at Milan, I do not. Do the same. Follow the custom of the Church where you are."

▶ SAINT AMBROSE

(328) Name the French peasant girl–now a saint–who witnessed the apparition of the Blessed Virgin Mary at Lourdes in 1858.

(329) Name the first Catholic president of the United States of America.

(330) This small Italian town–used by popes for their summer residence since the 17th century–is situated on the Alban Hills overlooking Lake Albano about thirty kilometers southeast of Rome. Name this town.

(331) In the early-14th century, the papacy was moved temporarily from Rome to which city, then part of the Kingdom of Naples and now part of modern-day France?

(332) Name the person to whom Mary appeared at Guadalupe, Mexico.

(333) Which famous Leonardo da Vinci painting–commissioned in 1495 and today housed in Milan, Italy–depicts Christ with the apostles at the Passover meal?

(334) Where was Pope John Paul II nearly assassinated by Turkish Bulgarian Mehmet Ali Ağca in 1981?

(335) Who is the first native-born citizen of the United States to be canonized (1975)?

(336) This English king is remembered for his struggles with the Church over his desired divorce from his wife, Catherine of Aragon, which led to his establishing the Anglican Church and separating from the Roman hierarchy. Name him.

(337) Which U.S. city has the most Catholics? (a) New York, (b) Los Angeles, (c) Miami, (d) San Antonio

(338) This Catholic university annually awards the Laetare Medal honoring distinguished service to country and Church. Name this university.

(339) Which American colony was originally founded–through the work of Lord Baltimore of England–as a safe haven for English Catholics?

(340) What is the first church in North America to be elevated–by Pope Pius IX in 1874–to the rank of basilica (minor)?

(341) Name the first ecumenical council–convoked in 325 A.D.–of the Catholic Church.

(342) What historic joint Catholic-Orthodox declaration did Pope Paul VI and Orthodox Ecumenical Patriarch Athenagoras I make in 1965?

(343) In 993, Pope John XV became the first pope to formally and universally canonize a saint in the way we know it today. Name this saint. (Hint: bishop)

(344) This Irish-Catholic American, dubbed "The Father of the American Navy," is credited with founding the United States Navy. Name him.

(345) What is the name for the military conflict between Catholics and Muslims in the Holy Land during the Middle Ages?

(346) What do James Nicholson, Francis Rooney, and Mary Ann Glendon share in common?

(347) What is the name for the bell tower of the Duomo, the magnificent cathedral in Pisa, Italy?

(348) Which meeting of Church leaders led to the elimination of the *Index Librorum Prohibitorum* ("List of Prohibited Books")?

(349) What is the name for an ecclesiastical province–equivalent to a diocese in the Latin Rite–within the Eastern Catholic Churches under the jurisdiction of an eparch–the equivalent of a bishop?

(350) This Eastern Catholic Church–lead by the "Patriarch of Babylon" based in Mosul, Iraq–comprises nearly 700,000 Christians and is centered in present-day Iraq with a large population in Southeast Michigan. Name this Church that maintains full communion with the Holy See.

(351) This person was both the first African-American Catholic priest and first African-American bishop. Name him.

(352) What honor was bestowed on the Tuscan Countess Matilda Canossa?

(353) Name the Eastern Catholic Church with the largest number of faithful followers.

(354) What significance does the date November 23, 1964 hold in the Catholic Church? (Hint: the Mass)

(355) This Irish American and member of the Knights of Columbus was the Democratic Party U.S. presidential candidate in 1928 (losing to Herbert Hoover) making him the first Roman Catholic to run for U.S. president as a major party nominee. Name him.

(356) The naval armada of this invading country was defeated by a Christian fleet of the Holy League at the Battle of Lepanto on October 7, 1571 thus staving off an invasion of Eastern Europe. Name this invader.

(357) The Counter Reformation was mobilized by which 16th century ecumenical council convened to define the differences between the Catholic and Protestant faiths with regards to formal teachings and traditions?

(358) Which continent has the largest population of Catholics and which continent has the fastest growing population of Catholics?

(359) Although assuming regnal names did not become commonplace until Pope Sergius IV (1009), this pope was the first pope to change his name and take a regnal name in A.D. 533. Name him.

CHAPTER 4

(360) In what year did Roman Catholics become the single largest religious denomination in the United States?

(361) Which United States presidential cabinet position was the first to be held by a Catholic in 1831?

CATHOLIC TOP 10

Largest Catholic Institutes of Women

	INSTITUTE	MEMBERSHIP
1	Salesian Sisters	14,665
2	Calced Carmelites	9,857
3	Claretians	7,463
4	Franciscan Missionaries of Mary	7,050
5	Franciscan Clarist Congregation	6,984
6	Sisters of the Mother of Carmel	6,428
7	Missionaries of Charity	5,046
8	Charity of St. Bartholomew of Capitanio	4,967
9	Benedictine Nuns	4,613
10	Perpetual Adorers of the Blessed Sacrament	4,583

Source: Catholic Almanac 2009

(362) How much larger is the global population of Catholics than the combined global population of Protestants?

(363) In 1858, the Blessed Virgin Mary appeared to the French girl Bernadette on eighteen separate occasions. Where did this occur?

(364) Where can you find the Diocese of Mackenzie-Fort Smith, the largest geographical Catholic diocese in the world?

(365) Who was the leader of the apostles and the first pope of the Church?

Ultimate Catholic Trivia

863 ► Saint Cyril and Saint Methodius sent to evangelize Slavic peoples.

(366) What was the name of the Catholic chaplain character in the popular television series *M*A*S*H*?

(367) In response to a deadly plague ravaging Italy during the 6th century, Pope Gregory the Great replaced the expression "Good luck to you," often said when someone sneezed (a sneeze was thought to be a precursor to a deadly illness), with what now common expression?

(368) Founded by the Society of Jesus in 1881, this Catholic university located in Milwaukee is the largest private university in Wisconsin. Name this university run by the Jesuits.

(369) Located approximately halfway between Libya and Sicily, this tiny independent island nation is ninety-nine percent Catholic, the highest percentage of any country. Name this nation.

Flag of the State of the Vatican City

(370) In which city was World Youth Day held in 2008?

(371) This distinguished Catholic university was founded in the 19th century by Father Edward Sorin and later lead by Father Ted Hesburgh. Name this Catholic university meaning "Our Lady."

(372) According to legend, to which present-day country did Joseph of Arimathea take the Holy Grail and spear with which Longinus pierced Christ's side?

(373) Which Protestant religion founder and leader did Pope Leo X excommunicate by papal bull *Decet Romanum Pontificem* on January 3, 1521?

(374) Which major American city is named for Saint Francis of Assisi?

(375) Located in South Orange, New Jersey, this Catholic university was founded by Archbishop James Roosevelt Bayley in 1856 making it the oldest diocesan university in the United States. Name this university.

(376) Ironically, after who is the town of Fátima, Portugal named?

(377) Name the only apostle–excluding Judas–not to be martyred.

(378) Which U.S. president re-established ties with the Holy See–ties that remain unbroken today?

(379) Name the very first Catholic Order native to the United States.

(380) This cross–containing images of people who have a part in the meaning of the Crucifixion–is the icon cross that Saint Francis of Assisi was praying before when he received the commission from the Lord to "rebuild the Church." Name this cross.

(381) During the 9th century, a collection of forged documents attributed to popes from Saint Clement (88–97) to Gregory II (714–731) were distributed. What are these documents called?

(382) Which saint was honored with his image on a U.S. 20-cent commemorative stamp issued in 1982?

(383) Name the diocese/archdiocese with the most Catholics in the world.

(384) In 1875, Filippo Cecchi–a 19th-century Catholic priest–invented a scientific instrument that monitors, measures, and records vibrations in the subsurface of the earth. What did he invent?

(385) Which present-day country became, in the early-16th century, the very first predominately Catholic land in Southeast Asia?

(386) According to estimates, Catholics of what ethnic heritage will comprise fifty percent of all Catholics in the United States by the year 2020?

(387) Where did three shepherd children witness six apparitions of the Blessed Virgin Mary in 1917?

IT HAPPENED IN 1582

▶ Named for Pope Gregory XIII, the Gregorian calendar, today's modern calendar, was put into effect and first adopted by Italy, Spain, and Portugal. This calendar was eventually adopted by most countries with England delaying adoption until 1752 and Turkey in 1926.

(388) On which day of the week was the Last Supper shared?

(389) In which century was the First Vatican Council convoked by Pope Pius IX?

(390) What solemnity celebrates the Blessed Virgin Mary, at the end of her earthly life, being taken up body and soul into heaven?

(391) This university president and Catholic priest defied more than eighty U.S. bishops and broke Church rules when he awarded U.S. President Obama—a strong pro-abortion supporter—an honorary doctorate of laws degree in 2009. Name this priest.

(392) Who are the six Catholic justices on the United States Supreme Court as of September 2009?

(393) In what year was Saint Peter's Basilica consecrated by Pope Urban VIII? (a) 1056, (b) 1401, (c) 1626, (d) 1729, (e) 1801

(394) In the early 1930s, nearly 7,000 Catholic clergy were killed during the "Red Terror." In which country did this occur?

(395) During the Depression, U.S. President Franklin D. Roosevelt criticized which controversial priest for his passionate radio broadcasts from the Shrine of the Little Flower in Royal Oak, Michigan?

(396) In 325, Roman Emperor Constantine convoked a council and made two decrees related to early Christianity. What are these two landmark decrees?

(397) This group of Catholics believes in the restoration of many or all of the liturgical forms, public and private devotions, and presentations of Catholic teachings which prevailed in the Church before the Second Vatican Council. Name this group.

(398) The Roman Pantheon, originally dedicated as the "Temple for All the Gods," was rededicated when Christianity became the official religion of the Roman Empire. To who was it rededicated?

(399) Appointed by Pope John XXIII in 1962, this person was the very first African cardinal in Catholic Church history. Name him.

(400) Name the very first Catholic university in the United States.

(401) This island–named for the mother of Roman Emperor Constantine and the person who, according to legend, discovered the True Cross used to crucify Christ–is the place where French General Napoleon Bonaparte died in 1821 after a six-year exile. Name this island.

(402) Name the very first pope to visit the Holy Land.

(403) What primary Catholic symbol was introduced only after the Protestant Reformation and not before?

(404) How many new members of the College of Cardinals did Pope John Paul II name in an unprecedented consistory in 2001?

(405) Which U.S. state has the highest percentage of Catholics and which the lowest percentage of Catholics?

(406) Founded in 1887, this Catholic university is the only university in the United States technically owned by Catholic bishops as it is independent of any religious order. Name this university.

(407) This cloth, presently housed in the Duomo di San Giovanni in Turin, Italy, was used to wrap Christ's body for burial. What is the name of this cloth?

(408) In which U.S. state do Cajun Catholics predominately live?

(409) Founded by the Diocese of New York in 1841 as Saint John's College, this Catholic university has three campuses located in and around New York City. Name this university.

(410) Name the popular Christmas song about a boy and his drum.

(411) What is the significance of the Epistle to the Smyrnaeans written by Saint Ignatius of Antioch to Christians in Smyrna around 106 A.D.?

(412) Which apparition of the Blessed Virgin Mary involved the Miracle of the Sun? (a) Beauraing, (b) Fátima, (c) Guadalupe, (d) Lourdes

(413) This person was the first American man and first American bishop to achieve sainthood. Name him.

(414) Located in Pittsburgh, Pennsylvania, this private Catholic university was founded by members of the Congregation of the Holy Spirit in 1878. Name this university.

(415) What is another name for an Iona Cross?

(416) This country has more Catholic colleges and universities than any other country in the world. Name this country.

(417) Which Broadway production by Victor Hugo was included in the *Index Librorum Prohibitorum* and thus banned?

(418) This cathedral, the oldest cathedral in North America, is the official cathedral for the Archdiocese of New Orleans. Name this cathedral.

(419) What support organization did Sister Mary Ignatia Gavin co-establish at the St. Thomas hospital in Akron, Ohio in 1939?

CHAPTER 4

(420) What is unique about the construction and engineering of the Basilica of the National Shrine of the Immaculate Conception on the campus of the Catholic University of America?

(421) According to tradition, how many apostles are buried in Rome?

(422) Which comedian was arrested at the Vatican for impersonating a Catholic priest?

(423) How many ecumenical councils has the Church convened throughout its history?

(424) In which state was the first Catholic parochial school established in the United States?

(425) In 1957, the communist regime of China established a semi-autonomous organization to lead the Catholic Church in that country in opposition to the Holy See. Name this organization.

(426) Today, people sometimes refer to an unusually warm September as "Indian summer." What was this type of weather called before Columbus discovered the New World?

(427) Of the thirty-three "Doctors of the Church," who are the three women?

(428) This veil is said to have the imprinted image of Christ's face received after the veil was used to wipe Christ's face while carrying the Cross. Name this famous veil.

> **IT HAPPENED IN 39 A.D.**
> ▶ Saint Peter baptized the Gentile Cornelius and his family signaling the mission of the Church to all peoples.

(429) What was the first language of divine worship in the Church and still the liturgical language of the Chaldean, Malabar, Malankar, Maronite, Nestorian, and Syrian Rites?

(430) In which country do the majority of Coptic Catholics live?

(431) Which major river in Canada–partly bordering the United States–is named for a saint?

(432) The ancient Romans were known for being tolerant of different religions and allowed freedom of worship. Why then did the Romans persecute the early Christians?

(433) Nearly 40,000 rare books were transported from this abbey to the Vatican for safe keeping before the battle there in World War II. Name this abbey.

(434) Which Italian Renaissance astronomer did Pope John Paul II exonerate in 1992?

(435) Which apostle was the first to be martyred?

(436) Where can you find Catholic fellowship organizations for residence and Catholic ministry called Newman Centers?

(437) In which century did the Catholic Church adopt Latin as its standard language?

(438) Although hotly debated, which musical chant developed by Pope Saint Gregory I in the 6th century is considered the beginning of Western music?

(439) Located in New Orleans, this private, coeducational, liberal arts university was founded for African-American Catholics in 1915. Name this university.

(440) Where did five children witness thirty-three apparitions of the Blessed Virgin Mary in 1932–1933?

(441) Pope Pius VI established the first Catholic diocese in the United States on April 6, 1789. Name the American city where this diocese was established.

(442) In 1728, the Ursuline Sisters established the first Catholic hospital in the (future) United States. In what city was the hospital established?

(443) According to ancient Catholic tradition, why do we cover our mouths when we yawn?

(444) Which Roman emperor was the last–yet bloodiest–to persecute Christians?

(445) Who was the first Catholic priest to be appointed Chaplain of the United States Senate?

(446) Despite petitions by priests to ban this drink given its Muslim origin, "the devil's drink" was approved by Pope Clement VIII who found it delicious and declared that "We shall cheat Satan by baptizing it." Name this drink.

(447) Although his great-uncle Constantine had legalized Christianity, this later Roman Emperor renounced his Christian faith and attempted, but failed, to outlaw Christianity. Name him.

(448) In which present-day country was the first Catholic diocese established in the New World in the early-16th century?

(449) What is the name for the underground cemeteries used by early Christians?

(450) This Christmas candy–shaped like a shepherd's crook–has alternating red and white stripes to represent the Lord's purity and sacrifice and is peppermint flavored to represent the royal gift of spice. Name this Christmas candy.

(451) What is the name for the great religious, social, and political upheaval from 1517 to 1648 that divided the Catholic Church and resulted in Protestantism?

(452) Pope Saint Leo persuaded what infamous "barbarian" leader to spare Rome in A.D. 452?

(453) What is the name given to a person who voluntarily suffers death for his faith or a Christian virtue?

(454) This Catholic Englishman–a writer, poet, philologist, and university professor–is best known as the author of *The Hobbit*, *The Lord of the Rings*, and *The Silmarillion*. Name him.

(455) Owing to early Jesuit missions, this city was the center of Japanese Catholicism before an atomic bomb devastated the city at the end of World War II. Name this city.

(456) The University of Notre Dame's administrative building is topped by the famous "Golden Dome." What statue rests atop this dome?

(457) In which European country did both the Advent wreath and the Christmas tree originate?

(458) The first Mass in the English-speaking American colonies was held on Saint Clement's Island on March 25, 1634. In which colony and future state was this Mass celebrated?

(459) As of 2009, what are the top three U.S. states with the most Catholics?

(460) Name the first Catholic bishop (1789) and archbishop in the United States.

(461) Who are the two patron saints of Canada?

(462) Where in France did an apparition of the Blessed Virgin Mary–followed by numerous accounts of miraculous healings–occur in 1846 to two shepherd children, Mélanie Calvat and Maximin Giraud?

CHAPTER 4

EVENTS, ORIGINS, AND MISCELLANEOUS

1171 ► Canonization of saints is officially reserved to the Holy See.

(463) What religious connection do Knute Rockne and Babe Ruth specifically share?

(464) Name the first Catholic diocese–created in 1576–in the Far East.

(465) Founded by Archbishop John F. Noll in 1912, this Roman Catholic publishing company prints a national weekly newspaper, Catholic magazines, and many books on Catholic topics. Name this publisher based in Huntington, Indiana.

(466) This Canadian city is home to more Catholics in Canada than any other city. Name this city.

(467) Which well-known hospital in the United States was founded by Lebanese-American Catholic entertainer Danny Thomas?

(468) According to medieval legend, whose bones are contained in the cathedral of Cologne, dubbed the "City of the Three Kings"?

(469) This French archbishop, founder of the Society of Saint Pius X, opposed changes associated with Vatican II and illicitly ordained four bishops. The Holy See immediately excommunicated him and the four bishops–although the four were reinstated by the Vatican in 2009. Name this former archbishop.

(470) This stadium in Rome was the site of many persecutions of early Christians. Name this stadium.

(471) "A.D." stands for Anno Domini in Latin. What does this translate to in English?

(472) Which major South American city has a towering 250-foot "Christ the Redeemer" statue of Jesus overlooking the city's bay from a mountain top?

(473) What was the name given to Pope Paul VI's policies towards the Soviet Union and other Eastern European countries with the aim of improving the living condition of Christians behind the Iron Curtain?

Ultimate Catholic Trivia

1182 ► Maronite Church reaffirms its communion with the Holy See.

(474) Approximately forty percent of Catholic clergy died from a plague that ravaged Europe during the 14th century. Name this plague.

(475) This powerful family from Renaissance Florence provided four popes to the Church. Name this family.

CATHOLIC TOP 10

Cardinal Electors by Country

	COUNTRY	CARDINALS
1	Italy	20
2	United States	13
3	Spain	6
4	France	6
5	Germany	5
6	Brazil	4
7	Poland	4
8	Mexico	4
9	India	3
10	Canada	3

As of February 2009

(476) This Catholic settlement is the oldest European-founded city in the United States. Name this city.

(477) In which country do Maronite Catholics, an Eastern Catholic Church, predominately live?

(478) John F. Kennedy, the first Catholic-American president and member of the Knights of Columbus, established which distinguished volunteer organization in 1961?

(479) In a dream, this Roman emperor saw—before his historic victory at the Battle of Mulvian Bridge in 313—a luminous cross in the sky with the words "In hoc signo vinces," meaning "In this sign you will conquer." Name him.

(480) According to legend, what house was transported from the Holy Land to its present site in Loreto, Italy?

(481) This once long-running musical featured the pre-Vatican II Catholic school experience. Name this musical.

(482) The very first apparition of the Blessed Virgin Mary appeared in 352 A.D. to an elderly couple requesting them to build a shrine on Rome's Esquiline Hill. Name this apparition.

___

(483) Which European nationality established the first ethnic–or national–parish in the United States? (Hint: Philadelphia)

(484) How many bullets struck Pope John Paul II during the 1981 assassination attempt?

(485) This person, a deacon stoned in Jerusalem during the first half of the 1st century, is considered the very first Christian martyr. Name him.

(486) In 1986, which language became the very first Native American language to be approved for translation for most parts of the Mass?

(487) Which modern legal structure is based on the twelve apostles and Christ? (Hint: Last Judgment)

(488) Name "The Four Great Fathers" of the Latin Church.

(489) What was the language of the first distinctly American Christmas carol?

(490) Of the fifty-six signers of the United States Declaration of Independence, who was the only Catholic and, incidentally, the longest-lived signatory?

(491) What was the relationship of the three children who witnessed the apparitions at Fátima?

> **IT HAPPENED IN 325**
>
> ▶ The Ecumenical Council of Nicaea is convened. Results of this council include formulation of the Nicene Creed, fixing the date of Easter Sunday, and adopting regulations regarding clerical discipline.

(492) What present-day expression was actually started in the 16th century for those people who did not switch from the Julian calendar to the Gregorian calendar, a change that resulted in skipping days on the calendar?

(493) In which present-day city did the Spanish Franciscans open the very first Catholic school in the (future) United States in 1606?

(494) Which two councils are considered the greatest ecumenical councils held in the West?

(495) Who was the first pope to address the United Nations General Assembly?

(496) How many Christian religions existed prior to the Protestant Reformation?

(497) What is the name for the very first council of the Church convoked in 50 A.D.?

(498) Which American cardinal presided over the inauguration of U.S. President John F. Kennedy?

(499) Although Christians were granted freedom of worship by Emperor Constantine, which emperor made Christianity the official religion of the Roman Empire in 380 A.D. by Edict of De Fide Catolica?

(500) This Panamanian general took refuge in the residence of the papal nuncio (Vatican ambassador) from U.S. troops during the 1989 invasion of Panama. Name this general.

(501) Who was the first saint of the Americas?

(502) In 1531, Juan Diego saw visions of Mary by the ruins of a shrine destroyed by the Spanish and renamed Guadalupe. To whom was the shrine originally dedicated?

(503) Which angel did the three shepherd children see before they witnessed the apparitions of the Blessed Virgin Mary at Fátima?

(504) In what year during the 20th century did we have three different popes?

(505) Name the first reigning pontiff to visit the United States.

(506) What is the largest diocese–not archdiocese–in the United States as measured by the number of Catholics?

CHAPTER
F·I·V·E

TEACHINGS, BELIEFS, AND STRUCTURE

A Look Inside What Defines the Church

“Jesus Christ is not valued at all until He is valued above all.”

▶ SAINT AUGUSTINE

“If you want peace, work for justice.”

▶ POPE PAUL VI

(507) The giving of money, food, and clothing to the poor that is free and done for love of God is referred to by what name?

(508) What is the name for the body of laws and regulations made by or adopted by ecclesiastical authority for the government of the Catholic Church and Catholic members?

(509) What is the most severe penalty where a person is banished from the Church?

Pope Pius XI

(510) What are the names for the different mysteries in a complete Rosary?

(511) What word describes a person who displays serious disrespect, violation, or injurious treatment of holy persons, places, and things consecrated by God?

(512) What is the name for the marks of the wounds on the feet and hands that resemble the Crucifixion of Christ?

(513) Joyful Mysteries, Sorrowful Mysteries, Glorious Mysteries, and Luminous Mysteries each have the same number of individual mysteries. How many individual mysteries does each one recognize?

(514) True/False: The Catholic Church teaches that people who do not know and accept the Church will *NOT* be saved.

(515) In which year did the Church permit Catholics to attend Saturday evening Mass to fulfill the Sunday obligation?

(516) Approximately how many dioceses are there in the Latin and Eastern Catholic Churches? (a) 1,000, (b) 2,000, (c) 3,000, (d) 4,000

TEACHINGS, BELIEFS, AND STRUCTURE

1305 ▶ Papacy moves from Rome to Avignon due to French influence.

(517) True/False: The pope is unable to sin personally due to the declaration of papal infallibility.

(518) What are the two types of sin?

(519) How many books comprise the Old Testament in the Catholic Bible?

(520) What term describes the relaxing of Church rules and laws in specific and limited circumstances?

(521) What is the meaning of the word "Gospel"?

(522) What do the Old Testament books Tobit, Judith, Wisdom, Sirach, Baruch, 1 Maccabees, and 2 Maccabees share in common?

(523) The literal meaning for this word is "witness." Name this word.

(524) What word describes the highest act of love and reverence shown to God alone?

(525) Religious instruction classes are often referred to as C.C.D. classes. What does C.C.D. stand for?

(526) True/False: The Ten Commandments are different for Catholics and many Protestant faiths.

(527) Which Catholic doctrine states that the Blessed Virgin Mary was preserved from original sin?

(528) True/False: The tradition of priestly celibacy is derived from Church law and not divine law.

(529) Wisdom, understanding, knowledge, and fortitude (courage) are four of the seven gifts of whom?

(530) What does a circle represent in Catholicism?

(531) The Resurrection, Ascension, Descent of the Holy Spirit, Assumption, and Crowning of the Blessed Virgin are recognized as the five _____ Mysteries of the Rosary.

(532) What is the name for a Catholic question and answer book that summarizes principles and beliefs of the Church?

(533) What is the name for the rules and directive precepts that guide the celebration of Mass and administration of the Sacraments?

(534) This eight-day week begins with Easter Sunday and ends the following Sunday. Name this week.

(535) What is the name for the list, or set of biblical books, considered by the Church to be divine revelation and authoritative as Sacred Scripture for both the Old Testament and New Testament whereby no other books are considered Sacred Scripture?

CATHOLIC TOP 10
Largest Latin and Eastern Church U.S. Archdioceses & Dioceses

	LOCATION	POPULATION
1	Los Angeles	4,212,887
2	New York	2,554,454
3	Chicago	2,342,000
4	Boston	1,871,667
5	Brooklyn	1,561,638
6	Detroit	1,478,231
7	Philadelphia	1,458,642
8	Rockville Centre	1,396,723
9	Newark	1,318,557
10	Galveston-Houston	1,300,000

Source: United States Conference of Catholic Bishops

(536) The unbroken chain of authority that extends from the first apostles to the bishops of present is referred to as what?

(537) What is the term for the ministry of an apostle?

(538) True/False: Catholics are permitted to receive Holy Communion more than once per day.

(539) What is the name for someone who claims that they do not know or are unable to know whether God exists?

(540) Finish this Beatitude: "Blessed are those who mourn, for they ____."

(541) Upon their conversion to Catholicism, clergymen from this Protestant religion may be ordained to the Catholic priesthood even if married. Name this religion.

(542) What is the First Joyful Mystery?

(543) What Catholic tradition provides a ceremonious welcome for the Infant Jesus at Christmas?

(544) How many Catholic bishops are also called "Patriarch"?

(545) How many choirs—or classes—of angels are recognized by the Catholic Church?

(546) What name is given to an official member of a parish or church community?

(547) The journey to a shrine or other holy site is referred to by what name?

(548) What is the process by which an individual becomes a member of the Catholic Church?

(549) Asking God for a special favor is called what?

> **IT HAPPENED IN 1054**
> ► Beginning of the Great Schism between the Eastern and Western Churches in response to mutual excommunications from each side. The ultimate result was the separation of Orthodox Churches from unity with the Holy See.

(550) What do the following share in common: Agony in the Garden, Scourging at the Pillar, Crowning with Thorns, Carrying of the Cross, and the Crucifixion?

(551) What does the word "Alleluia," a word derived from Hebrew, mean?

(552) This Hebrew word means "It is true" or "So be it; truly." What is this word?

(553) According to the Beatitudes, what will the peacemakers be called?

1387 ► **Lithuanians are the last people in Europe to accept Catholicism.**

(554) According to the Code of Canon Law, how often are Catholics obligated to receive Holy Communion?

(555) True/False: Catholics are permitted to read non-Catholic editions of the Bible only if two requirements are fulfilled–they must be involved in Scripture study and the Bible edition does not attack the Catholic faith.

(556) According to tradition, what did ringing a bell, closing a book, and extinguishing a candle represent?

(557) Clothing the naked, caring for the sick, feeding the hungry, and sheltering the homeless are four of the seven works of what?

(558) According to tradition, the death of a pope is verified when the cardinal camerlengo (papal chamberlain) calls out three times with no response from the pope. What specifically does the cardinal call out?

(559) True/False: The King James Bible is an approved Catholic edition.

(560) Finish this Beatitude: "Blessed are the meek, for they _____."

(561) An action, word, offense, or desire contrary to the will of God is best defined as what?

(562) In Christian artwork, Christ and saints are commonly depicted with circles of light above their heads. What are these circles of light called?

(563) How many Eastern Catholic Churches are in full communion with the Holy See?

(564) According to Catholic tradition, what does an anchor symbolize?

(565) According to the Code of Canon Law, what is the penalty for "a person who actually procures an abortion"?

(566) What is the name for the suffering, death, Resurrection, and Glorification of the Lord?

CHAPTER 5

TEACHINGS, BELIEFS, AND STRUCTURE

1412 ► Saint Joan of Arc has visions telling her to lead her countrymen.

(567) This title is given to a saint from whose writings the Church derived a great advantage and to whom "eminent learning" and "great sanctity" have been attributed by a proclamation of a pope or of an ecumenical council. Name this title.

(568) What do the eight points of the Maltese Cross represent?

(569) Acts of self-discipline involving prayer, hardship, austerities, and penance are referred to as what?

(570) According to tradition, which angel with a flaming sword guards the gate to the Garden of Eden?

(571) Prior to the Second Vatican Council, what was the name for the Holy Spirit?

(572) For a person to be beatified, how many miracles must be proven to have taken place through the intercession of the person being considered?

Saint John Neumann

(573) What is the name given to a school supported and operated by a parish community?

(574) Fill in the blank: Pride, lust, envy, and anger are four of the Seven _____ Sins.

(575) What is the name for supernatural truths the Church teaches that are above reason and comprehension?

(576) What sin, literally meaning "the worship of idols," does one commit by worshiping something or someone other than God?

(577) What change did Pope Paul VI approve to the Stations of the Cross in 1975?

(578) This fabled bird is symbolic of the Resurrection. Name this bird.

(579) What term describes the sharing of faith through witness of life and word?

(580) This type of Mass is celebrated in honor of some mystery of the faith or of a saint or all the saints and not according to a feast on the calendar. Name this type of Mass.

(581) How many individual small scapulars are approved by the Church?

(582) What is the term used to describe the denial of the existence of God the Father?

(583) What is the First Glorious Mystery?

IT HAPPENED IN 1528

▶ The Order of Friars Minor Capuchin is approved as an autonomous branch of the Franciscan Order. Much of the early work performed by this organization centered on the Counter Reformation.

(584) What is the theological term for the mystery that Jesus is both wholly God and wholly human?

(585) Any form of active Catholic service is best referred to by what name?

(586) What is the name for the group of people baptized into the Church, but not ordained or consecrated to the religious state?

(587) A pontifical college is more commonly known by what other name?

(588) According to the *Catechism of the Catholic Church*, this term describes a process–not a place–of purification after death for those who are saved to ensure that they may achieve the holiness necessary to enter heaven. What is this term?

(589) What is the name for a council whereby bishops from around the world gather in order to make solemn decisions for the universal Church?

(590) What is the First Sorrowful Mystery?

(591) What is the name for the gifts of divine spiritual graces given an individual or group for the good and spiritual welfare of the community or Church?

(592) What are the three theological virtues of the Catholic Church?

(593) Although the Holy See recognizes ten Holy Days of Obligation, the United States only recognizes six. What are the missing four holy days? (Hint: two were moved to the nearest Sunday and two were removed from the list altogether)

(594) According to the Code of Canon Law, what are the four major sins against the Fifth Commandment, "You Shall Not Kill"?

(595) Name the three persons of the Holy Trinity.

(596) What is the name for an ecclesiastical jurisdiction and territory governed by an archbishop?

(597) What does Canon Law require be enclosed in every Catholic church and chapel?

Papal Coat of Arms

(598) This event is best defined as "an observable event on earth that cannot be explained by natural laws." As a result, this event is considered an Act of God by the Catholic Church. What specifically is this event?

(599) What do the following three elements share in common: grievous matter, sufficient reflection, and full consent of the will?

(600) What is the holiest night of the year in the Catholic Church?

(601) How many books comprise the New Testament in the Catholic Bible?

(602) What two items can be consumed without breaking the Eucharistic fast?

CATHOLIC TOP 10

Countries with the Most Priests

	COUNTRY	PRIESTS
1	Italy	50,148
2	USA	44,906
3	Poland	28,457
4	Spain	25,281
5	France	21,930
6	India	19,946
7	Germany	18,365
8	Brazil	16,853
9	Mexico	14,618
10	Canada	8,441

Compiled by: Catholic-hierarchy.org from official Vatican sources

(603) What is the name for the science or branch of theology that is concerned with the defense of Catholic doctrines?

(604) What is the belief that a person only needs to rely upon God's goodness for salvation?

(605) What color scapular–worn by members of the Confraternity of Our Lady of Mt. Carmel–is the most celebrated of all scapulars?

(606) This title, the first of four steps toward possible canonization, is given to a deceased person whose life and works are being investigated in consideration for official recognition by the pope and the Church. Name this title.

(607) What Italian word for the Blessed Virgin Mary means "My Lady"?

(608) This process, initiated by a legally divorced person, requests the Church to declare nullity, or not valid, a sacramental marriage. Name this process.

(609) Established in 10th-century England where land owners were taxed a penny, this annual and now voluntary donation from the faithful of various countries helps to defray expenses of the Holy See. Name this donation.

(610) The word "Catholic" comes from the Greek word "katholikos," meaning what?

(611) The "Four Marks" of the Church represent a summary of the most important affirmations of the Catholic faith. Name these Four Marks. (Hint: Nicene Creed)

(612) An assembly of cardinals presided over by the pope is referred to by what name?

(613) What do the "Dolors" commemorate in the Seven Dolors of Mary?

(614) The word "Beatitude" is derived from the Latin word "beatus," meaning what?

(615) What are the Four Cardinal Virtues?

(616) Holy Communion given to those in danger of death is referred to by what name meaning "provision for a journey" in Latin?

> **IT HAPPENED IN 1809**
>
> ▶ After capturing Italy and the Papal States, Napoleon deports Pope Pius VII to France and imprisons him there. While in captivity Pope Pius VII refuses to cooperate with Napoleon who wants to bring the Church under French control. Pope Pius remained in exile until 1814.

(617) How many of the twenty-one ecumenical councils do both the Roman Catholic Church and Orthodox Church agree as being mutually valid?

(618) This process is the act of reducing an ecclesiastical person or thing to a lay status, such as releasing an ordained person from his ministry or transitioning a church building to a secular purpose. Name this process.

(619) An expression of insult or contempt with respect to God is referred to as what?

(620) This term means giving one-tenth (10%) of one's income to the Church. What is this term?

(621) According to tradition, what are the three triads, or levels, of celestial hierarchy in the choir of angels?

CHAPTER S·I·X

SEASONS, HOLY DAYS, AND THE MASS

Examining How We Worship as Catholics

❝The culmination of the Mass is not the Consecration, but Communion.**❞**

▶ **SAINT MAXIMILIAN KOLBE**

❝Holy Communion is the shortest and safest way to Heaven.**❞**

▶ **POPE SAINT PIUS X**

(622) What is the name for the cup containing the Precious Blood of Christ at Mass?

(623) What holy day commemorates the Holy Spirit descending on the apostles celebrated fifty days after Easter?

(624) On which three body parts do Catholics make small signs of the cross before the Gospel is proclaimed?

(625) This term, derived from the Latin word for "I will wash," refers to ritual washing of the thumbs and index fingers of the celebrant at Mass. Name this term.

(626) This type of holy day is the highest liturgical rank of any holy day in the ecclesiastical calendar with seventeen such days celebrated in the Church. Name this type of holy day.

(627) What is the first day of Lent called?

(628) The eve of a feast day is referred to by what name?

(629) What is the name for the rope-like belt–signifying chastity–worn by a priest over the alb and around his waist?

(630) On which holy day did Jesus rise from the dead to life?

(631) What is the Greek translation for "Lord have mercy"?

(632) Name the basin for holding baptismal water in a church.

(633) Weekday Mass readings are cycled every two years. How often are Sunday Mass readings cycled?

(634) This day is the only day of the liturgical year without a celebration of the Eucharist. Name this day where the religious service includes Holy Communion that is "pre-sanctified," meaning consecrated the night before.

(635) What symbol on a Catholic calendar represents a Day of Abstinence whereby eating meat is prohibited?

(636) Which bird can be seen drinking from a chalice in many traditional Christian artworks?

(637) This part of the Mass comprises the presentation of the gifts, Eucharistic prayer, and Holy Communion. Name this part of the Mass.

(638) Which hymn recited by the congregation ends with the word "highest," thus signaling all to kneel?

(639) In which month is the final Sunday of the liturgical year?

(640) What is Christ often depicted pointing to in Christian artwork?

Pope Benedict XV

(641) Candles used in many Church functions—particularly Sacraments—should contain at least fifty percent of what component?

(642) What solemnity is celebrated on the last Sunday in the western liturgical calendar?

(643) On what holy day do some Catholics bless their homes and inscribe the names of the three Magi with white chalk on the inside door frame?

(644) What is the name for the incense burner hanging from chains used at Mass?

(645) This person is charged with the care of the sacristy, sacred vessels, vestments, and other articles required for any liturgical function. Name the title of this person.

(646) During Ordinary Time, the second readings for Mass are taken from what two authors?

(647) What does a priest or Eucharistic minister say before giving the Eucharist to the communicant?

(648) What is the name for the body-length white liturgical robe or tunic—signifying innocence—worn by priests during Mass?

(649) In the liturgical calendar, are there more movable feast days, immovable feast days, or feasts assigned to Sundays?

(650) Which large candle—often deposited with five grains of incense to symbolize the five wounds of Christ—is lighted during the Easter Vigil and remains lit throughout the Easter liturgical season until extinguished after the Gospel on Ascension Day and then removed?

(651) What is the name given to the days—other than Sundays—on which the faithful are required to attend Mass?

(652) Once called the Feast of the Incarnation, this solemnity celebrates the event when Mary was visited by Gabriel the Archangel and asked to be the mother of Jesus. Name this solemnity.

(653) When is Trinity Sunday (also called Most Holy Trinity) celebrated?

(654) Which optional memorial was established by the Church to counter the communist May Day celebration by offering a Christian view of work?

(655) This stiff square piece of linen—sometimes decorated with a cross or other embroidery—is used to cover the chalice to safeguard against impurities. Name this linen.

(656) This motion symbolizes the Cross on Calvary by tracing the shape of a cross in the air or on one's own body. Name this motion.

(657) How many Masses during the liturgical year honor the Blessed Virgin Mary?

(658) Although its use is optional, this bell is rung when the Sacred Host is elevated at the Consecration during Mass. Name this bell.

(659) This book is one of several ritual books for the administration of the Sacraments or other liturgical offices as well as an annual calendar containing abbreviated directions for daily Mass. Name this book.

(660) What is the Church's dedication for the month of July?

(661) This form of prayer consists of invocations by a priest or deacon with responses from the congregation. Name this form of prayer.

(662) What is the Church's dedication for the month of December?

(663) During which liturgical season should Catholics abstain from eating meat on Fridays?

(664) With what should Catholics sign themselves when entering or leaving a church or chapel?

(665) True/False: Priests must say preparatory prayers called access prayers before celebrating Mass.

(666) What kind of bread is required to make Eucharistic hosts in the Latin Church?

(667) What is the name given to a Mass in which two priests celebrate together?

> **IT HAPPENED IN 1215**
>
> ▶ The Ecumenical Council of the Lateran (IV) is convened. This council ordered annual reception of the Sacraments of Reconciliation and Holy Communion and introduced the official use of the term transubstantiation to explain the changing of the bread and wine into the Precious Body and Blood.

(668) Which important solemnity–celebrating the Incarnation of Our Savior–is celebrated by the Church nine months before Christmas–typically on March 25th (but sometimes on March 26th)?

(669) Laetare Sunday is the fourth Sunday in which liturgical season?

(670) What is the name for the third Sunday in Advent when the pink candle of the Advent Wreath is lighted?

(671) What is an Anticipated Mass?

(672) During what two liturgical seasons is the Gloria not recited?

(673) Name the side table used at Mass to hold the bread and wine.

(674) What is the name for the step or floor on which the altar rests?

(675) For what reason do Catholics make a small sign of the cross on their lips (in addition to the forehead and heart) before hearing the Gospel?

(676) In what year were lay ministers first permitted to distribute the Eucharist?

(677) What is the name for an ornamental canopy above an altar?

(678) Who reads the first and second readings at Mass?

(679) Rubrics are typically associated with which color font in the Missal or other liturgical books?

(680) What solemnity celebrates the birthday of the Church?

(681) This case or boxlike receptacle is used for the exclusive reservation of the Blessed Sacrament of consecrated bread and wine. What is it?

(682) True/False: Lectors are permitted to read the Gospel if preceded by a blessing from a priest.

(683) What optional memorial, attracting more than three million people over eleven days in September, is celebrated in New York City to honor the patron saint of Naples, Italy?

(684) This dish was traditionally held by an altar boy during reception of the Eucharist under the chin of the communicant to catch any particle of the Sacred Host that may fall. Name this dish.

(685) What gesture should U.S. Catholics perform right before receiving the Eucharist as a sign of reverence acknowledging Christ's presence?

(686) What liturgical color–symbolic of humility, sorrow, and penitence–is used during Advent and Lent?

(687) What is the name for the section of a church that contains the baptismal font and surrounding area?

(688) What is the name for the candles lit in front of statues in churches?

(689) The flat top of a consecrated altar is referred to by what name?

(690) What is another name for a vestibule leading to a nave in a church building?

(691) The Service of Light is the first service held during which vigil?

(692) What is the Church's dedication for the month of October?

(693) These small bottles or vessels contain the water and wine used at the Consecration. Name these small bottles.

Reputed burial place of Saint Patrick at Downpatrick, Ireland

(694) What is burnt to produce the ashes for Ash Wednesday?

(695) Which musical instrument is most commonly found in churches?

(696) What solemnity celebrated on November 1st commemorates all saints, known and unknown, who do not have individual feast days?

(697) What is the name for the watch-shaped container used to transport the Eucharist to the sick or homebound?

(698) What is the liturgical color–symbolic of hope–used during Ordinary Time?

(699) What does a priest say prior to the congregation saying "We lift them up to the Lord"?

(700) Established by the Council of Nicaea in 325, the date for which solemnity is determined by the new vernal equinox?

(701) This box–labeled O.S. for olea sancta (holy oils)–holds the holy oils and is commonly found on the wall or recess in the wall of the sanctuary. Name this box.

(702) What major change to the Sunday readings was instituted when the New Lectionary was introduced in 1970?

(703) A conopaeum is a veil used to cover what item?

IT HAPPENED IN 1962-1965

▶ The Ecumenical Council of the Vatican (II) is convened by Pope John XXIII with the intent to renew and reform the Church. Sixteen documents were formulated and promulgated as a result of the council. The council was closed by Pope Paul VI.

(704) How many actual days comprise the forty days of Lent?

(705) This vessel or plate–usually made of silver or gold–holds the priest's Sacred Host during the Liturgy of the Eucharist. Name this item.

(706) Holy Wednesday, the day of Judas Iscariot's first conspiratorial meeting with the Sanhedrin to betray Jesus, is known in some parts of the Catholic world by another name. What is this name?

(707) This garment, worn in processions or when attending but not celebrating services, is a voluminous ecclesiastical vestment with a long train, proper to cardinals, bishops, and certain other honorary prelates. Name this garment.

(708) Resembling a chalice, this cup is used to hold the Sacred Hosts which will be used for Holy Communion. Name this cup.

(709) What is the name for the two-handed vessel with a long neck used to hold holy oils?

(710) What is the name for the chief singer of an ecclesiastical choir who typically selects the music for the liturgy?

(711) How many Sacred Scripture passages from the Bible are typically read during each Mass?

(712) Which holy day commemorates the rising to heaven of Christ's body and soul on the fortieth day after the Resurrection?

(713) What does a priest kiss when he begins and ends Mass?

(714) What is another name for a sermon?

(715) What is the generic name for the hymn sung at the conclusion of Mass?

(716) Which Catholic solemnity immediately follows Halloween?

(717) The New Roman Missal was revised in 1974. Approximately how many years had it been since the last revision?

(718) This part of the Mass comprises the readings, responses, Gospel, and homily. Name this part of the Mass.

(719) True/False: All wine used in the Eucharist must be fermented.

(720) What is the name for the liturgical practice of dipping the Sacred Host into the consecrated wine before consumption?

(721) Which year marked the first time in which parishioners in the United States were allowed to receive the Eucharist in the hand?

(722) This hymn is sung or recited in place of the Angelus during the Easter season. Name this hymn.

(723) What are the three liturgical occasions when ashes are used ceremoniously?

(724) What does the Church call, although not widely used in the United States, the day before Ash Wednesday, also known as Pączki Day or Fat Tuesday?

(725) True/False: Eucharist and Holy Communion mean the same thing.

(726) Fill in the blank: "I believe in the Holy Spirit, the Holy Catholic Church, the Communion of Saints, the forgiveness of sins, the Resurrection of the body, and _____. Amen."

(727) What colors are the candles of an Advent Wreath?

(728) What is the name for the seats in a church used by the congregation?

(729) This room is where clergy vest for ecclesiastical functions and where sacred vessels, vestments, and other articles needed for liturgical use are stored. Name this room.

(730) With what does each litany begin?

(731) This book includes both the Sacramentary (ritual part of the Mass) used only by the celebrant and the Lectionary (readings from Sacred Scripture) for the celebrant and assisting ministers. Name this book.

(732) Which prayer precedes the Liturgy of the Word?

(733) Which Church-wide memorial and feast day proper to the United States is celebrated on December 12th?

(734) On which date does the Church celebrate the World Day of Peace?

CHAPTER 6

(735) The Feast of the Transfiguration is celebrated during which month?

(736) What is the name for the square white linen cloth on which the chalice and paten are placed at Mass?

(737) This feast day celebrating the family unit and the family of Jesus (Jesus, Mary, and Joseph) falls on the Sunday after Christmas. Name this feast day.

(738) What is the name for the center part of a church from the lobby area to the altar surrounded by aisles?

(739) This book contains psalms and prayers for the congregation. Name this book.

(740) What is the name for the banner or curtain hanging in front of an altar?

(741) What is the name for the basin in the sacristy which drains directly into the earth for the fitting disposal of blessed ashes, oils, and holy water?

(742) What is the response from the congregation to the words from a priest at Mass, "The Lord be with you"?

(743) Name the liturgical season that prepares Catholics for Christmas.

(744) What is the appropriate response from the congregation during the Prayers of the Faithful?

(745) What does a priest or deacon say at the conclusion of each Mass?

(746) What is the name for the consecrated area in a church where the altar is found—often enclosed by a lattice or railing?

(747) Dr. Joel Poinsett, the U.S. ambassador to Mexico in the early-19th century, brought back to America a plant referred to by Mexicans as the "flower for the Holy Night." Name this flower now synonymous with Christmas.

(748) This term describes the official public worship, service, duty, or work–distinguishable from private devotion–of the Church faithful. What is this term?

(749) How often does a Holy Year or a Jubilee–a special year of remission of sins and universal pardon generally involving pilgrimage to a sacred site–occur in the Catholic Church?

(750) Which candle can always be found lit in a Catholic church to signify the presence of the Blessed Sacrament?

(751) This flower is symbolic of Easter and is sometimes entwined on an Easter Cross. Name this flower.

CATHOLIC TOP 10

Popes with the Shortest Reigns

	POPE	PONTIFICATE
1	Urban VII	13 days
2	Boniface VI	16 days
3	Celestine IV	17 days
4	Theodore II	20 days
5	Sisinnius	21 days
6	Marcellus II	22 days
7	Damasus II	24 days
T8	Pius III	27 days
T8	Leo XI	27 days
10	Benedict V	33 days

(752) When Mass is offered "pro popolo," what does this mean?

(753) What term describes the changing of bread and wine into the Precious Body and Blood of Christ? (Hint: not Consecration)

(754) Which liturgical book contains hymns, offers, and prayers for the canonical hours?

(755) This holy day commemorates Christ's manifestation to the gentiles in the person of the Magi, as well as His baptism and first miracle at Cana. Name this holy day.

(756) Name the white linen cloth used to wipe the chalice after each communicant partakes.

CHAPTER 6

(757) What is the name for the small white linen towel used by priests to dry their hands after the ablution and prior to the Consecration?

(758) What is the name for the instrument used to sprinkle holy water on the congregation at Mass?

(759) What is the name for the group of people who lead the congregation in singing at the liturgy?

(760) The name for this liturgical season is taken from the Old English word for spring-tide and the Saxon name for March, "Lenctenid." Name this liturgical season.

(761) This holy day is commonly symbolized by an egg for its representation of new life. Name this holy day.

(762) A day of partial abstinence—meaning meat is permitted only once per day—is represented by what image on a Catholic calendar?

(763) What is the name for the week beginning with Palm Sunday and ending with Holy Saturday?

(764) What is the first solemnity celebrated in the liturgical year?

(765) What solemnity—held on June 29th—is celebrated when a large floral display resembling a fisherman's net is hung between two columns at Saint Peter's?

(766) What is the name for the booth-like room used by priests for the administration of the Sacrament of Reconciliation?

(767) What is the name for the container that holds relics?

(768) This tradition was started during medieval times when the eating of eggs was forbidden during Lenten fasting. What is this modern tradition?

(769) The Nuptial Blessing is given by the priest after the congregation recites which prayer?

(770) What is the name for the portable metallic bucket for holding holy water used in blessings?

(771) What is the name for a kneeling bench–resembling a wooden desk–mainly intended for private devotions?

(772) What is the name for the three-day period that begins with the Mass of the Lord's Supper on Holy Thursday and concludes on the evening of Easter Sunday?

(773) What is the Church's dedication for the month of January?

(774) Name the sleeveless outer garment worn by priests at Mass.

(775) During the Easter and Christmas liturgical seasons, the second readings are taken from what two authors?

(776) During what part of the Mass are palms blessed on Palm Sunday?

(777) Holy Chrism, oil used for the administration of certain Sacraments, is a mixture of what two ingredients?

(778) What is the vessel used for ritually washing the celebrant's thumb and index finders at ablution?

(779) Rank the following holy days beginning with the most important: feast, memorial, and solemnity.

CHAPTER
S·E·V·E·N

SACRAMENTS, SACRAMENTALS, AND PRAYERS

All About Sacred Catholic Traditions and Customs

"What was visible in Christ has now passed over into the Sacraments of the Church."

▶ **POPE SAINT LEO THE GREAT**

"Prayer is the best weapon we possess, the key that opens the heart of God."

▶ **SAINT PADRE PIO**

(780) Which prayer devoted to Mary consists of multiple Hail Marys and Our Fathers through meditation of God's mysteries?

(781) What is the Latin translation for the Hail Mary?

(782) What color scapular commemorates the Seven Sorrows of Mary?

(783) What is the name for the "walk" that Catholics commemorate to retrace Christ's journey to Calvary?

CATHOLIC TOP 10

U.S. States with the Most Catholics

	STATE	CATHOLICS
1	California	10,382,988
2	New York	7,166,308
3	Texas	6,586,240
4	Illinois	3,871,047
5	New Jersey	3,562,389
6	Pennsylvania	3,530,817
7	Massachusetts	2,709,552
8	Florida	2,366,715
9	Michigan	2,216,372
10	Ohio	2,068,348

Source: Catholic Almanac 2009

(784) This Sacrament is typically for people who are in danger of death or experiencing serious illness. Name this Sacrament.

(785) Who is the "originating minister" for the Sacrament of Confirmation?

(786) Which Sacrament joins the person to the passion of Christ, gives power, peace, and courage to endure suffering, forgives sins, restores health, and prepares for the passage to eternal life?

(787) What are best described as outward signs of inward grace, instituted by Christ for our sanctification?

(788) What color scapular commemorates the Immaculate Conception?

(789) This perfumed oil—consecrated by a bishop at a special Mass on or near Holy Thursday—signifies the gift of the Holy Spirit to the one being anointed. Name this oil.

SACRAMENTS, SACRAMENTALS, AND PRAYERS

1720 ► The Passionists are founded by Saint Paul of the Cross.

(790) What are sacred signs that extend and radiate the Sacraments, signifying the mostly spiritual effects obtained through the Church's intercession and disposing a person to the grace of the Sacraments?

(791) Salve Regina is another name for which prayer?

(792) Which type of sin can only be absolved through the Sacrament of Reconciliation?

(793) This Marian prayer, the most popular non-liturgical devotion, is considered "an abridgement of the whole Gospel." Name this prayer.

(794) What are the two Sacraments of Service?

(795) What is the act in which a priest grants forgiveness?

(796) What color scapular commemorates the Passion of Our Lord?

(797) What does salt symbolize in the Sacrament of Baptism?

(798) Which Sacrament is characterized by the parable of the Prodigal Son?

(799) What is the name for the uninterrupted hour of prayer in presence of the Blessed Sacrament?

(800) Aside from holy water, what are the three ingredients of "Gregorian Water" used to consecrate a church?

(801) According to the Code of Canon Law, what is the minimum age requirement for baptismal sponsors?

(802) Which finger does a priest use when administering the Sacrament of Anointing of the Sick?

(803) What is the name for the perfumed oil used during the Sacraments of Baptism, Confirmation, and Holy Orders?

(804) What is the First Station of the Cross?

(805) How many mysteries are recognized in the Rosary?

(806) What is the name for nine days of public or private prayer for a special occasion or intention?

(807) Which Sacrament uses the liturgical posture of "prostration," or lying face down?

(808) How many Hail Marys comprise a complete fifteen decade Rosary?

(809) According to the Church, what are the only linens (material) acceptable for use as an altar cloth?

(810) At what age may Catholics receive the Sacrament of Anointing of the Sick?

(811) Complete the title of this hymn: Mother _____, Mother Fairest.

(812) What is the name for a person seeking initiation into the Church and a candidate for Baptism?

(813) True/False: Openness to the procreation and education of children is required for a marriage to be a Sacrament.

(814) When a person receives the Sacrament of Anointing of the Sick, what other two Sacraments are commonly received at the same time?

(815) Mentioned by Saint Basil in the 4th century and prescribed by Pope Gregory the Great in 590, this litany is considered the most ancient of all Church litanies. Name this litany.

(816) The words "taken from among men" are attributed to which of the seven Sacraments?

(817) Which litany begins with the words, "Lord, have mercy on us"?

CHAPTER 7

(818) True/False: Any person, regardless of religion, may baptize another into the Catholic faith in cases of necessity.

(819) What sin does the Sacrament of Baptism remove?

(820) What prayer did Jesus give the apostles after they asked Him to teach them how to pray?

(821) Name the three levels or degrees of the Sacrament of Holy Orders.

(822) Ascribed to the apostles, this Creed is a formula of belief containing the fundamental doctrines of Christianity in twelve articles. Name this Creed.

(823) The Solemnity of Pentecost is perpetuated in the Church through which Sacrament?

(824) What is the act by which a Catholic professes his sins to a priest during the Sacrament of Reconciliation?

(825) What do the following saints share in common: Saint Mary Magdalene, Saint Agatha, Saint Lucy, Saint Agnes, Saint Cecily, Saint Catherine, and Saint Anastasia?

> **IT HAPPENED IN 100 A.D.**
>
> ► The Age of the Apostles and the first generation of the Church ends with the death of Saint John the apostle and evangelist.

(826) What was the first Creed in which the equality of the three persons of the Holy Trinity was explicitly stated? (a) Apostles' Creed, (b) Athanasian Creed , (c) Nicene Creed, (d) Trentine Creed

(827) How many months are holy oils kept for use?

(828) Which Sacrament is symbolized by a dove?

(829) This detailed statement or summary of the Catholic faith was drafted by the first two ecumenical councils–Nicaea in 325 and Constantinople in 381. Name this Creed.

(830) Which prayer begins with the words, "Remember, O most gracious Virgin Mary"?

(831) This prayer, recited at the beginning of Mass, is a Catholic prayer of penance wherein sinfulness is acknowledged by the faithful. Name this prayer beginning with "I confess to almighty God…"

(832) Which Sacrament is symbolized by grapes and wheat?

(833) What daily devotion to the Blessed Virgin Mary commemorates the Incarnation of Christ?

(834) What is the Fourth Station of the Cross?

(835) Which prayer is typically used to commemorate the Seven Dolors of Mary?

(836) In the Sacrament of Baptism, what does water symbolize?

(837) What three Sacraments cannot be repeated as they impart an indelible spiritual mark?

(838) How many sponsors are required for the Sacrament of Baptism?

(839) Which Sacrament is symbolized by a cross with two circles?

(840) On what part of the body does the bishop anoint with oil during the Sacrament of Confirmation?

(841) In 2002, Pope John Paul II announced five new optional mysteries to the Rosary bringing the total number of mysteries to twenty. What is the name for these optional mysteries?

(842) True/False: Although wedding rings are a common part of the marriage ceremony, they are not part of the Sacrament of Matrimony.

(843) Which Sacrament is symbolized by two candles?

(844) What are the three valid methods for administering the Sacrament of Baptism?

(845) Which Sacrament was once called "Extreme Unction," meaning "Final Anointing"?

(846) According to the Code of Canon Law, what is the minimum age requirement for a valid marriage?

(847) Only two of the four Gospels contain petitions included in the Our Father. Name these two Gospels.

(848) Sponsors for the Sacrament of Baptism are known by what more common name?

(849) What is the English title for the hymn Adeste Fidelis?

(850) What are the two Sacraments of Healing?

(851) The Hail Mary is based on two passages from the Gospel of Luke. Name these two Gospel passages.

(852) While reciting the Angelus, how many times do you pray the Hail Mary?

(853) What term is defined as a prayerful appeal to a higher power–God, angels, or saints–for supernatural assistance?

(854) How many promises does the Blessed Virgin Mary offer to those who pray the Rosary?

(855) Catechumenate is the process of preparation for which Sacrament?

(856) What is the difference between a crucifix and a cross?

(857) Name all Seven Sacraments of the Catholic Church.

(858) According to the Code of Canon Law, how often are Catholics obligated to confess their sins to a priest through the Sacrament of Reconciliation?

(859) Fill in the blank: Saint Francis of Assisi wrote the prayer titled Lord, Make me an _____.

(860) Which prayer is commonly prayed during confession as a sign of true sorrow for sin and the desire to receive God's forgiveness?

Maltese Cross

(861) What is the Second Station of the Cross?

(862) How many Stations of the Cross are there?

(863) When would a woman receive a "Churching of Woman" blessing?

(864) Which geometric shape is the favored form for a baptismal font?

(865) Penance, absolution, and confession all refer to which Sacrament?

(866) Which Sacrament initiates a person into the Church?

(867) How many Sacraments may a woman receive?

(868) What is the name used in the Eastern Catholic Rite to signify Confirmation?

(869) Praying for the interests of others rather than ourselves is referred to by what name?

(870) What are the three Sacraments of Initiation?

(871) Housed at Trinity College in Dublin, Ireland, this 8th-century book is an ornately-illustrated manuscript of the Latin Gospels created by Irish monks. Name this well-known book.

CHAPTER 7

SACRAMENTS, SACRAMENTALS, AND PRAYERS

1858 ▶ Blessed Virgin Mary appears to Bernadette at Lourdes, France.

(872) What Creed begins with "I believe in God, the Father Almighty"?

(873) Name the container used to display the Sacred Host during Eucharistic adoration or Benediction of the Blessed Sacrament.

(874) Which two Sacraments cannot be received by the same person in nearly all cases?

(875) What is the Thirteenth Station of the Cross?

(876) When praying the Rosary, how many times do you pray the Hail Mary after announcing a mystery and then praying one Our Father?

(877) Which Sacrament confers on a man the grace and spiritual power to consecrate the Eucharist and to sanctify others?

(878) What is the Fourteenth Station of the Cross?

(879) True/False: Anointing of the Sick is reserved for those who are at the point of death.

(880) Which two Sacraments are administered by bishops rather than by priests?

(881) Incense, candles, scapulars, rosaries, and missals are referred to as what kind of religious items?

(882) What is the form of Baptism called when the entire body is submerged under water?

(883) What color scapular commemorates the Holy Trinity?

> **IT HAPPENED IN 529**
>
> ▶ The Abbey of Monte Cassino–located in present-day Italy–was established by Saint Benedict of Nursia. This abbey is one of the few remaining territorial abbeys within the Catholic Church.

(884) Praying all fifteen decades of a traditional Rosary is called what?

(885) This prayer is typically the final prayer recited when praying the Rosary. Name this prayer.

(886) This Creed, created in response to the Arian heresy, is the only Christian Creed accepted in common as authoritative by the Catholic, Orthodox, Anglican, and other major Protestant faiths. Name this Creed.

(887) The Angelical Salutation is another name for which prayer?

CHAPTER
E·I·G·H·T

ORGANIZATIONS, ORDERS, AND CLERGY

Discovering the Who's Who of Church Leadership

"Lord, help me to preach the Gospel wherever I go, and if I must, even through words."

▶ SAINT FRANCIS OF ASSISI

"We cannot do great things in life: we can only do small things with great love."

▶ BLESSED TERESA OF CALCUTTA

(888) What is the name for the long scarf-like liturgical vestment–worn over the alb–that distinguishes a priest from a deacon according to how it is worn?

(889) Founded by Father Michael J. McGivney in New Haven, Connecticut, this organization is the largest Catholic fraternal service organization in the world. Name this organization with nearly two million members and 14,000 councils worldwide.

(890) Born Rita Antoinette Rizzo on April 20, 1923, this nun entered the Poor Clares of Perpetual Adoration, a Franciscan Order for women, in 1944. However, she is best known as the founder of the *Eternal Word Television Network*. Name her.

(891) What is the official name for the Dominican Order?

(892) What are the five Mendicant Orders?

(893) Born Agnesë Gonxhe Bojaxhiu on August 26, 1910 in Macedonia (then part of the Ottoman Empire), this Catholic nun founded the Missionaries of Charity in 1950. By what other name is she known?

(894) Which clergymen wear the stole over the left shoulder and joined at the hip?

(895) What are the three religious vows taken by consecrated monastic men and women of the Church?

(896) This rank of ordination is open to married men. Name this ordination.

(897) What is the name for the long robes once commonly worn by Catholic sisters?

(898) Which clergymen are responsible for ordaining bishops, priests, and deacons?

(899) What is the title for the person that directs a seminary?

(900) What is the traditional residence of Catholic religious women called?

(901) Cardinals gained their distinctive colored garment and hat under the reign of Pope Innocent IV (1243–1254). What color–symbolic of ones willingness to shed blood for his faith–is the garment and hat?

(902) The leader of this Order is referred to as the "Black Pope" for his significant influence in the Church and for wearing black vestments in contrast to the pope who typically wears white vestments. Name this Order.

(903) Founded in 1943 by U.S. bishops, this organization is the international humanitarian agency of the Catholic community in the United States. Name this organization that provides relief and developmental programs to eighty million people in more than 100 countries.

(904) What is the title for a female superior of a monastic community?

(905) What is a dalmatic?

(906) What is the title for someone acting in the name and with the authority of another person in the exercise of a clerical office?

(907) Originated by the Benedictines, this outer garment consists of two strips of cloth joined across the shoulders and worn by members of certain Orders. Name this garment.

Seal of the Society of Jesus

(908) What is another name for a nun's bedroom?

(909) This congregation of Catholic priests and lay brothers live together in a community bound together by no formal vows–only the bond of charity. Name this congregation.

(910) Born on May 25, 1887 in the town of Pietrelcina, Italy, I am known for having received the stigmata on numerous occasions with the first such stigmata occurring on September 20, 1918. Who am I?

(911) Founded in 1966, this organization is the official leadership body of the Roman Catholic Church in the United States and is composed of all members of the Catholic hierarchy in America. Name this organization.

(912) Name the three colleges/universities located in Indiana that are run by the Congregation of Holy Cross.

(913) What is the name for a regular assistant bishop–without personal jurisdiction–under the leadership of a diocesan bishop?

(914) What Catholic Order is traditionally in charge of Vatican Radio?

IT HAPPENED IN 754

▶ Pepin, father of Charlemagne, was crowed ruler of the Franks by Pope Stephen II (III). Pepin twice came to the aid of the pope to defend against the Lombards.

(915) This Catholic Order was founded in Italy by Saint Angela Merici in 1535 primarily for the education of girls and the care of the sick and needy. Name what is today the oldest teaching Order for women in the Catholic Church.

(916) Priests who are not members of religious orders are referred to by what name?

(917) Which two different Catholic Orders use the initials S.J. and O.S.B. after their names when being formal?

(918) This large-sleeved liturgical tunic, commonly worn by clergy during processions and when administering the Sacraments, is made of white linen or cotton material. What is this tunic called?

(919) Which organization awards the Cardinal Spellman Award honoring a Catholic for outstanding achievement in theology?

1918 ▶ The Code of Cannon Law goes into effect in the Western Church.

(920) What is the age whereby bishops and archbishops must submit their resignations for retirement to the pope?

(921) What is the name for the geographical region or district under the leadership of a local bishop?

(922) On what finger do popes, cardinals, bishops, nuns, and other clergy wear their religious rings?

(923) This person, a Bavarian Roman Catholic nun, served as housekeeper and confidant to Pope Pius XII with some claiming that she was the real power within the Vatican. Name her.

(924) Fill in the blanks: Members of Mendicant Orders are referred to as _____ while members of Cenobite (Monastic) Orders are referred to as _____ .

(925) What is the name for the skullcap–called "pileolus" in Latin– sometimes worn by Catholic clergymen?

(926) This organization is one of the largest lay-run apostolates in the United States. In addition to publishing the *This Rock*, it also publishes *The Official Catholic Directory* and produces a live radio show called *Catholic Answers Live*. Name this organization.

(927) What is the minimum age requirement for married men to be ordained permanent deacons?

(928) What religious Order did Saint John Bosco establish in 1859 to care for the young and poor children of the industrial revolution?

(929) In which city did the Missionaries of Charity (Mother Teresa's Order) establish their first convent in the United States?

(930) What charism, or spiritual focus, are the Carmelites principally engaged?

(931) Who was the Catholic priest known for his work with lepers in Hawaii, specifically the island of Molokai?

(932) This bishop was a renowned theologian earning the Cardinal Mercier Prize for International Philosophy in 1923. He hosted the radio program *The Catholic Hour* (1930–1950) and won an Emmy Award for Most Outstanding Television Personality. Name this bishop whose cause for canonization was opened in 2002.

CATHOLIC TOP 10

Largest Catholic Institutes of Men

	INSTITUTE	MEMBERSHIP
1	Jesuits	19,216
2	Salesians	16,389
3	Franciscans (Friars Minor)	15,256
4	Franciscans (Capuchins)	11,166
5	Benedictines	7,640
6	Society of the Divine Word	6,096
7	Dominicans	6,044
8	Redemptorists	5,601
9	Brothers of Christians Schools	5,473
10	Oblates of Mary Immaculate	4,548

Source: Catholic Almanac 2009

(933) What does C.Y.O., an organization established in Chicago, stand for?

(934) Which lay minister is responsible for helping teach children in the ways of prayer and the essentials of Catholic faith and morals?

(935) What is the female equivalent of a monk?

(936) Which clergymen wear purple skullcaps?

(937) Which clergymen have the ecclesiastical title of "His Eminence"?

(938) Founded in 1973, this U.S. organization is the nation's largest Catholic civil rights organization defending the rights of Catholics– lay and clergy alike–to participate in American public life without defamation or discrimination. Name this organization.

(939) Which clergymen have the ecclesiastical title of "His Excellency"?

(940) Which magazine does the Redemptorist Fathers publish?

(941) This French-born priest and delegate from Michigan Territory was the first Catholic priest to serve in the United States House of Representatives. Name this priest.

(942) What do the three knots of a cincture represent?

(943) What is the name for a nun who has not yet taken her vows?

(944) What does R.C.I.A. stand for?

(945) What is the title for the person who oversees members of a Catholic Order?

(946) Which Catholic Order, officially known as the Society of Jesus, has the motto, "To the greater honor and glory of God"?

(947) What respected weekly national magazine, established in 1909, do the Jesuits publish?

(948) What is the name for the dining room in a monastery or convent called?

(949) According to tradition, this Order was established by Saint Berthold around the 12th century on Mount Carmel in present-day Israel. Name this Order.

(950) In which year was Mother Teresa awarded the Nobel Peace Prize?

(951) What is the common name for the hood of a religious habit?

(952) What is the name for the black outer coat worn by a bishop?

(953) This liturgical article of clothing–used to distinguish archbishops from bishops–is made from the wool of two lambs–one symbolizing Christ as the Lamb of God and the other symbolizing Christ as the Good Shepherd. Name this liturgical article of clothing.

(954) In which country did Mother Teresa primarily work?

(955) What is the name for the house in which the parish priest resides?

Father Michael J. McGivney

(956) Who are considered the successors of the apostles in communion with the pope?

(957) True/False: Married candidates for the permanent diaconate must receive their wives consent to the ordination.

(958) Where was the Society of Saint Vincent de Paul founded by Blessed Frédéric Ozanam in 1833?

(959) Catholics in the United States comprise about six percent of all Catholics worldwide. However, what percentage of all permanent deacons reside in the United States?

(960) What word, derived from the Greek word "episkopos," means "overseer"?

(961) This Catholic Order is recognized as the greatest promoter of the Rosary. Name this Order.

(962) What now-common word originated from a Catholic order–founded by Italian cleric Lambert le Bègue–who lived entirely on donations they solicited from the public?

CHAPTER 8

(963) What is the name for an auxiliary bishop with right to succession?

(964) This liturgical headdress–worn by popes, cardinals, bishops, and abbots–is a folding two-pieced stiffened cap of silk or linen, typically richly ornamented with gold embroidery. Name this headdress.

(965) This vow is a promise to God not to engage in sexual activity or to marry. Name this vow.

(966) True/False: Unmarried permanent deacons must remain celibate.

(967) What is the ethnic heritage of the majority of American bishops? (a) German, (b) Irish, (c) Italian, (d) Latino, (e) Polish

(968) What 17th-century French Benedictine monk was an important quality pioneer for Champagne wine but who, contrary to popular myths, did not discover the champagne method for making sparkling wines?

(969) What is the meaning of the word "deacon"?

(970) This Cenobite, or Monastic Order, refers to those religious institutes who have inherited the spirit of Saint Basil. Name this Order that has produced fourteen popes, 1,800 bishops, 3,000 abbots, and 11,000 martyrs.

(971) This Order, also called the Catholic Foreign Mission Society of America, emphasizes ministry and missionary work overseas with more than 550 priests and brothers serving in various countries around the world. Name this Order.

(972) This magazine, one of the largest Catholic family magazines in the United States, was first published by the Franciscan Friars of Cincinnati in 1893. Name this well-known magazine.

(973) Which Catholic Order produces the famed blue Ermite cheese?

(974) The Mother of Good Counsel scapular is promoted by which Order?

(975) How many bishops are typically required to ordain a new bishop?

(976) This ornamental staff, shaped like a shepherd's crook, is carried by or before a bishop as a symbol of his authority. What is this staff called?

(977) What ecclesiastical and honorary title, translating to "My Lord," is sometimes bestowed on priests as a mark of papal recognition?

(978) This priest, born in Ireland in 1886 and granted American citizenship in 1919, founded Boys Town, arguably the most famous orphanage and center for troubled boys in America. Name this man whose life was made famous by the 1938 film *Boys Town* starring Spencer Tracy.

(979) According to the *2009 Catholic Almanac*, approximately how many priests are there in the United States as of 2008?

(980) What is the name for the necklace cross worn by popes, cardinals, archbishops, bishops, and some abbots and abbesses?

(981) This saint, the patron saint of astronomers and the Dominican Republic, was the founder of the Order of Preachers (Dominicans). Name him.

(982) This independent news organization is staffed by lay Catholic journalists dedicated to providing accurate world news written from a distinctively Catholic perspective. Name this news organization.

(983) What is the name used for several Catholic orders and congregations taken in honor and under the patronage of Saint Paul the Hermit?

(984) Who founded the Order of Poor Ladies, the second Franciscan Order to be established?

(985) In 1967, Pope Paul VI restored the role of which clergymen in the Latin Rite and placed the decision regarding its local restoration in the hands of each nation's Episcopal Conference?

(986) True/False: Members of the Society of Saint Vincent de Paul are lay persons rather than clergymen.

CHAPTER 8

ORGANIZATIONS, ORDERS, AND CLERGY

1939-45 ▶ Convents, monasteries, and the Vatican are used to hide Jews.

(987) Originating in the 14th century largely as a result of the Black Death, this group of saints is venerated together because their intercession was thought to be particularly effective, especially against various diseases. Name this group.

(988) Founded by the Vincentians in 1898, this university of over 23,000 students takes its name from a 17th-century French priest who valued philanthropy. Name this university considered the largest Catholic university and one of the ten largest private universities in the United States.

(989) What is the title for a priest appointed for pastoral service in the military?

(990) Fill in the blanks: A _____ is a female monastic that predominately lives a contemplative life of prayer and meditation within a monastery while a _____ is a female monastic that predominately lives an active vocation of service to the needy, sick, poor, and uneducated.

(991) This full-length, fitted robe for ordinary use is colored black for priests, purple for bishops, red for cardinals, and white for popes. Name this robe.

(992) When a pope, archbishop, or patriarch dies, what is done with his pallium?

Pope Paul VI and U.S. President John F. Kennedy

(993) Which Catholic Order did Lúcia Santos, one of the three shepherd children who witnessed the apparition of the Blessed Virgin Mary at Fátima, join in 1948?

1950 ▶ Tomb of Saint Peter identified underneath Saint Peter's Basilica.

(994) What Order–approved by Pope Benedict XIII in 1725–did Saint Paul of the Cross establish?

(995) This Order of Catholic women was founded by Catherine McAuley in Dublin, Ireland in 1831. Name this Order with about 10,000 members worldwide.

(996) What is the name for the white headdress worn under the veil of a Catholic nun?

(997) What religion did the Franciscan Friars of the Atonement practice before their conversion to Catholicism?

(998) This cable network–the largest religious cable network in the world–transmits Catholic programming twenty-four hours a day to more than fifty-five million homes in thirty-eight countries and territories. Name this cable network.

(999) Which clergymen have the ecclesiastical title of "His Holiness"?

(1000) When was the Knights of Columbus established by Fr. Michael J. McGivney? (a) 1671, (b) 1792, (c) 1866, (d) 1882

(1001) What do Father Robert J. Cornell, Father Robert F. Drinan, and Father Gabriel Richard share in common?

CHAPTER
N·I·N·E

ANSWERS

"If you do not hope, you will not find what is beyond your hope."

▶ SAINT CLEMENT OF ALEXANDRIA

"You cannot be half a saint. You must be a whole saint or no saint at all."

▶ SAINT THERESA OF LISIEUX

Chapter 1

(1) Gospels

(2) Pontius Pilate

(3) Matthew, Mark, Luke, and John

(4) Bethlehem

(5) Calvary

(6) Passover

(7) Sanhedrin

(8) Egypt

(9) Epistle

(10) Joseph of Arimathea

(11) Reed

(12) Saint Peter

(13) Three

(14) Blindness

(15) Saint Luke

(16) Two, James the Greater (son of Zebedee) and James the Less (son of Alphaeus)

(17) Criminals crucified with Christ

(18) Nicodemus

(19) Holy Grail

(20) Sea of Galilee (called the Sea of Tiberias by the Romans)

(21) Saint Paul (called the Pauline epistles)

(22) Death of friend Lazarus

(23) Saint Matthias

(24) Money changers and dove sellers

(25) Star of Bethlehem

(26) Wife of Pontius Pilate

(27) Mary Magdalene

(28) Shepherds

(29) Abba

(30) Paralysis

(31) Simon of Cyrene

(32) Devine inspiration

(33) Forty

(34) Savior

(35) Thorns (Crown of Thorns)

(36) Nazareth

(37) Second cousins

(38) Mary Magdalene

(39) Three Magi

(40) Three hours

(41) Finding Jesus preaching in the temple

(42) Matthew and Luke

(43) Luke

(44) Three

(45) (b) Jordan River

(46) Eye for an eye

(47) "Jesus of Nazareth, King of the Jews"

(48) Restored her to life

(49) "I will build my Church"

(50) Mount Tabor

(51) Anointed One

(52) Vulgate (Latin for "common")

(53) Ten, One

(54) They cast lots

(55) Apostles are "sent" while disciples are "called"

(56) Gospel of Mark

(57) To register for the Roman census

(58) That you should love the Lord your God with your whole heart, your whole soul, and with all your mind

(59) Acts of the Apostles

(60) Isaiah

(61) Sermon on the Mount

(62) Aramaic

(63) Gethsemane

(64) Parable

(65) Head of John the Baptist

(66) On the road to Emmaus

(67) Tongues of Fire

(68) The Visitation

(69) Matthew (28), Luke (24), John (21), and Mark (16)

(70) James, Peter, and John

(71) Lazarus

(72) Mary (that she would give birth to Jesus)

(73) Moses and Elijah

(74) John the Baptist

(75) Longinus

(76) Desert

(77) Turkey (Republic of)

(78) Christ's triumphant entry into Jerusalem

(79) Greek (specifically Koine Greek)

(80) Gospel of Matthew

(81) "make you fishers of men."

(82) Barabbas

(83) Dove

(84) Temple curtain

(85) A collection of books

(86) Seventy times seven (not just seven)

(87)   Latin, Greek, and Hebrew

(88)   Mary Magdalene

(89)   Judas

(90)   Wedding feast of Cana

(91)   Last Supper

(92)   "Doubting Thomas"

(93)   Thirty silver coins

(94)   Matthew, Mark, and Luke

(95)   Gold, Frankincense, and Myrrh

(96)   Feeding the multitude (also known as the miracle of the loaves and fish)

(97)   Three Magi from the East who visited the Infant Jesus

Chapter 2

(98)   Saint Catherine of Siena (1347–1380)

(99)   Formal names adopted by popes

(100) Pontificate

(101) Seven (three biblical and four from tradition)

(102) Shamrock

(103) Pope John Paul II

(104) Saint Benedict of Nursia (480–543)

(105) Saint Nicholas (of Myra, Asia Minor)

(106) Our Lady of Guadalupe

(107) Dominions

(108) Saint Cecilia of Rome

(109) Popes Pius XII (1958) and Paul VI (1978)

(110) Guardian Angel

(111) Michael, Raphael, and Gabriel

(112) (a) Father (or papa)

(113) Twice

(114) Pope John XXIII (1881–1963)

(115) Saint Ignatius of Loyola (1491–1556)

(116) Saint Francis of Assisi (1181–1226)

(117) Pope John Paul II

(118) Rosary

(119) Karol Józef Wojtyla

(120) Papal bull (or apostolic bull)

(121) St. Bernard (Saint Bernard of Menthon)

(122) Secret ballot

(123) Saint Augustine

(124) Saint Joan of Arc

(125) Pope Linus (from Tuscia, Italy)

(126) Blessed Virgin Mary

(127) Keys (Crossed)

(128) Thirty-four days

(129) Saint Agatha

(130) Saint Blaise

(131) Encyclical

(132) (a) 1946 (All Saints' Day)

(133) Pope Leo XIII (1810–1903)

(134) Saint Matthew

(135) Cherubim

(136) Pope Pius IX and Pope John XXIII

(137) Saint Augustine

(138) Eggs Benedict

(139) Relics

(140) Saint Anthony of Padua (1195–1231)

(141) Saint John Vianney (1786–1859)

(142) Pope John Paul II

(143) Saint Vincent de Paul

(144) Pope Pius X (Pontificate: 1903–1914)

(145) Saint Francis of Assisi (1181–1226)

(146) All abdicated as popes

(147) First Bishop of Rome to use the title "Pope"

(148) Saint Rose of Lima (1586–1617)

(149) Pope Adrian IV (Pontificate: 1154–1159)

(150) Communism

(151) Twenty-six years and five months

(152) Pope Pius XI

(153) Confessor (not to be confused with confessor priest)

(154) Saint Thomas More (Sir Thomas More)

(155) Angels

(156) Ring of the Fisherman or Fisherman's Ring

(157) Pope John Paul II

(158) Mother Frances Xavier Cabrini (1850–1917)

(159) Saint Andrew

(160) Germany

(161) Pope Pius IX (Pontificate: 1846–1878)

(162) Pope Benedict XVI (German), Pope John Paul II (Polish), and Pope Adrian VI (Dutch)

(163) First Native American beatified (1980)

(164) Saint Thomas Aquinas (1225–1274)

(165) Saint Patrick (387–461)

(166) Pope Gregory XIII (Gregorian calendar)

(167) Michael the Archangel

(168) Yes, Pope Saint Peter

(169) Church of San Domenico in Naples

(170) Benedictine Order

(171) Saint Peter

(172) John (last was Pope John XXIII)

(173) Children

(174) Saint Nicholas (Santa Claus)

(175) Pope John XXIII (1881–1963)

(176) Saint Thomas More

(177) Adolph Hitler

(178) Pope John Paul I

(179) Saint Thérèse of Lisieux (1873–1897)

(180) Pope John Paul II

(181) Immaculate Conception

(182) Teachers

(183) Saint Joachim (Father of the Blessed Virgin Mary)

(184) Saint Joseph

(185) Seven

(186) Last pope to use his birth name instead of adopting a regnal name

(187) Saint Maximilian Kolbe

(188) Pope Urban VII (reigned in 1590)

(189) Canonization

(190) Pope John Paul II, a big soccer fan

(191) Current site of Saint Peter's Basilica

(192) Pope John XXIII and Pope Paul VI

(193) Saint Thomas Aquinas (1225–1274)

(194) Ceremoniously smashed with a hammer by the papal chamberlain

(195) Sword

(196) 11th century

(197) Saint Jerome (c.347–420)

(198) Saint Francis of Assisi (1181–1226)

(199) South Korea

(200) Saint Aidan of Lindisfarne

(201) One of the bullets that struck him in the 1981 assassination attempt

(202) Saint Brendan of Clonfert (c.484–c.577)

(203) Saint Gerard Majella (1726–1755)

(204) 1978

(205) Saint Scholastica

(206) One who is like God

(207) March 17th

(208) Pope Paul VI (Pontificate: 1963–1978)

(209) Winged Man

(210) *The Jeweler's Shop*

(211) Lion

(212) Saint Anthony of Padua (1195–1231)

(213) Pope John XXIII (1881–1963)

Chapter 3

(214) Lateran Palace

(215) Michelangelo

(216) Diocese of Rome, the pope himself, and sometimes the officers in the papal government

(217) Cathedral

(218) 265

(219) List of nearly 4,000 forbidden and censored books

(220) Swiss Guard

(221) Basilica of Our Lady of Guadalupe

(222) Antipope

(223) No salary, nor a bank account

(224) Gold and white

(225) True, but Catholic clergy manage it for the Church

(226) Abbey

(227) Pope John Paul I

(228) Saint Peter's Basilica

(229) Magisterium

(230) Roman Rota

(231) Over sixteen miles

(232) Forty-four

(233) Only ATM in the world with instructions in Latin

(234) The Last Judgment

(235) White line on the pavement

(236) German

(237) Administrative office of a diocese

(238) Basilica of the National Shrine of the Immaculate Conception

1965 ▶ Joint Catholic-Orthodox declaration lifts mutual excommunication.

(239) Church of the Holy Sepulcher (Jerusalem)

(240) (Supreme Tribunal of the) Apostolic Signatura

(241) Ireland

(242) Scala Sancta (Holy Stairs)

(243) Supreme Order of Christ

(244) Two years, nine months, and two days

(245) Cathedral of Notre-Dame of Paris

(246) False (His pontificate begins upon his accepting the election results)

(247) 826

(248) College of Cardinals

(249) Westminster Abbey

(250) Apostolic nuncio (also known as papal nuncio)

(251) 110 plus six officers

(252) Guglielmo Marconi (1874–1937)

(253) Pope John XX

(254) 147

(255) Automatic and immediate excommunication

(256) No set official language

(257) Saint Peter's Square

(258) Two-thirds majority

(259) Eighty

(260) Treaty of Lateran Pacts

(261) Apostolic Palace

(262) Apostolic brief

(263) Ecclesiastical Latin

(264) Saint Stephen of the Abyssinians Church

(265) Six

(266) Cardinal protodeacon (the senior-ranking cardinal deacon)

(267) Lourdes

(268) True

(269) 1931

(270) 3,000

(271) Basilica of Saint John Lateran

(272) No official time limit

(273) Multiplying the loaves and fish

(274) Centuries of kissing by pilgrims

(275) 109 acres

(276) Saint Anne's

(277) Mar Emmanuel III Cardinal Delly

(278) Popemobile

(279) Shrine of the Most Blessed Sacrament

(280) (c) 456 years

(281) Two (the first was an antipope in the early-15th century)

(282) India

(283) Daily Vatican newspaper distributed to over 100 countries

(284) Jesuit

(285) Saint Catherine of Sienna

(286) Day of prayer

(287) Yellow, red, and blue

(288) Brazil

(289) Master of the Sacred Palace

(290) Papal Cross

(291) Conclave (Conclave of Cardinals)

(292) Servant of God, Venerable, Blessed, and Saint

(293) Christmas, Easter, Solemnity of Saints Peter and Paul, and at "Urbi et Orbi" blessings

(294) Cardinal secretary of state

(295) *Acta Apostolicae Sedis* (*Acts of the Apostolic See*)

(296) Rogito

(297) Vicar apostolic

(298) Interregnum or Sede Vacante (Vacant Seat)

(299) Papal Zouaves

(300) La Pietà

(301) Saint Valentine

(302) 120

(303) Saint Peter's Square

(304) Ring bells

(305) Castel Gandolfo

(306) Periti

(307) His tongue

(308) Ninety-one

(309) Roman Curia

(310) Sealed with keys, ribbons, and wax

(311) True

(312) Pikes and halberds

(313) One of only two square country flags in the world (the other being the flag of Switzerland)

(314) Hungry

(315) Pope Sixtus IV

(316) Cathedra

(317) "Laudetur Jesus Christus" ("Praised be Jesus Christ")

(318) Papal Tiara

(319) 150,000

(320) Chamberlain (camerlengo in Latin)

(321) True (it is not the seat of a bishop and therefore is not a cathedral)

(322) Lourdes

(323) French and Greek

(324) Quirinal Palace

(325) Gold stars on a blue background

(326) Ballots cast and straw

(327) 267 (Pope Benedict IX reigned three different times between 1032 and 1048)

Chapter 4

(328) Saint Bernadette Soubirous (1844–1879)

(329) John F. Kennedy

(330) Castel Gandolfo

(331) Avignon

(332) Juan Diego

(333) The Last Supper

(334) Saint Peter's Square

(335) Saint Elizabeth Ann Bayley Seton (1774–1821)

(336) King Henry VIII

(337) (b) Los Angeles

(338) University of Notre Dame

(339) Maryland

(340) Notre-Dame de Québec Cathedral

(341) First Council of Nicaea

(342) Lifted the 1,000 year old mutual excommunication resulting from the Great Schism of 1054

(343) German Bishop Ulrich of Augsburg (890–973)

(344) John Barry (1745–1803)

(345) The Crusades

(346) Former United States Ambassadors to the Holy See

(347) Leaning Tower of Pisa

(348) Second Vatican Council

(349) Eparchy

(350) Chaldean Catholic Church

(351) James Augustine Healy (1830–1900)

(352) First woman buried at Saint Peter's Basilica

(353) Byzantine (over eight million)

(354) Last day for mandatory Latin Mass

(355) Alfred E. Smith (1873–1944)

(356) Ottoman Turks

(357) Council of Trent

ANSWERS

1973 ▶ Marian apparitions in Japan—now known as Our Lady of Akita.

(358) South America has the largest and Africa is the fastest growing

(359) Pope John II (Mercurius)

(360) 1850

(361) Attorney General

(362) Greater than 2 to 1

(363) Lourdes, France

(364) Canada (predominately the Northwest Territories)

(365) Saint Peter

(366) Father Mulcahey

(367) "God Bless You"

(368) Marquette University

(369) Malta

(370) Sydney, Australia

(371) University of Notre Dame

(372) England

(373) Martin Luther

(374) San Francisco

(375) Seton Hall University

(376) Daughter of Mohammed (founder of Islam)

(377) Saint John

(378) President Ronald Reagan

(379) Sisters of Charity of Saint Joseph

(380) San Damiano Cross

(381) False Decretals

(382) Saint Francis of Assisi (1181–1226)

(383) Mexico City

(384) Modern seismograph

(385) The Philippines

(386) Latino/Hispanic

(387) Fátima, Portugal

(388) Thursday (Holy Thursday)

(389) 19th century

(390) The Assumption

(391) Father John Jenkins (University of Notre Dame)

(392) John Roberts (Chief Justice), Anthony Kennedy, Antonin Scalia, Clarence Thomas, Samuel Alito, and Sonia Sotomayor

(393) (c) 1626

(394) Spain

(395) Fr. Charles E. Coughlin

(396) Easter Sunday falls on the first Sunday after the full moon and the cross is the official symbol of Christianity

(397) Traditionalist Catholics

(398) Virgin Mary

(399) Lauren Cardinal Rugambwa

(400) Georgetown University, founded in 1789

(401) St. Helena's Island

(402) Pope Paul VI (in 1964)

(403) Crucifix

(404) Forty-four

(405) 1st: Rhode Island (59%) and 50th: Mississippi (7%)

(406) The Catholic University of America

(407) Shroud of Turin

(408) Louisiana

(409) Fordham University

(410) *The Little Drummer Boy*

(411) Earliest surviving witness to the use of "Catholic" to describe the whole Church

(412) (b) Fátima

(413) John N. Neumann (1811–1860), fourth Bishop of Philadelphia

(414) Duquesne University

(415) Celtic Cross

(416) United States (over 200)

(417) *Les Miserable's*

(418) Saint Louis Cathedral

(419) Alcoholics Anonymous

(420) Like medieval cathedrals, it is constructed entirely of masonry with no steel structure

(421) Seven (Bartholomew, James the Less, Jude, Matthias, Peter, Philip, and Simon)

(422) Don Novello, who played Father Guido Sarducci on the television comedy *Saturday Night Live*

(423) Twenty-one

(424) Maryland

(425) Patriotic Association of Chinese Catholics

(426) Saint Augustine's summer

(427) Saint Catherine of Siena, Saint Teresa of Avila, and Saint Therese of Lisieux

(428) Veronica's Veil

(429) Aramaic

(430) Egypt

(431) Saint Lawrence River

(432) Christians refused to worship Roman emperors as gods

(433) Monte Cassino

(434) Galileo Galilei

(435) Saint James the Greater, son of Zebedee

CHAPTER 9

ANSWERS

1977 ▶ John N. Neumann becomes the first American man canonized.

(436) Non-Catholic universities throughout the world

(437) 3rd century

(438) Gregorian chant

(439) Xavier University

(440) Beauraing, Belgium

(441) Baltimore

(442) New Orleans

(443) According to superstition, that's where and when a demon entered a person

(444) Diocletian

(445) Father Charles Constantine Pise (in 1832)

(446) Coffee

(447) Julian the Apostate

(448) Haiti

(449) Catacombs

(450) Candy cane

(451) (Protestant) Reformation

(452) Attila the Hun

(453) Martyr

(454) J. R. R. Tolkien (1892–1973)

(455) Nagasaki

(456) Statue of Mary

(457) Germany

(458) Maryland (beginning of the Archdiocese of Washington)

(459) (1) California, (2) New York, (3) Texas

(460) Bishop John Carroll

(461) Saints Joseph and Anne

(462) La Salette (Our Lady of La Salette)

(463) Converts to Catholicism

(464) Macau (present-day China)

(465) Our Sunday Visitor

(466) Montreal

(467) Saint Jude Children's Research Hospital

(468) Three Magi from the East who visited the Infant Jesus

(469) Marcel-François Lefebvre (1905–1991)

(470) Colosseum

(471) In the Year of Our Lord

(472) Rio de Janeiro, Brazil

(473) Ostpolitik

(474) Black Death

(475) Medici

(476) St. Augustine, Florida

(477) Lebanon

(478) Peace Corps

(479) Constantine

(480) Reputed Nazareth house of Mary

(481) *Do Black Patent Leather Shoes Really Reflect Up?*

(482) Our Lady of the Snows

(483) Germans (Holy Trinity German National Parish)

(484) Four

(485) Saint Stephen

(486) Navajo (followed by Choctaw in 1987)

(487) A twelve member jury and one judge

(488) Saint Ambrose, Saint Augustine, Saint Gregory (I) the Great, and Saint Jerome

(489) Huron (Native American)

(490) Charles Carroll (1737–1832), of Maryland

(491) Sister, brother, and cousin

(492) April Fools

(493) St. Augustine, Florida

(494) Council of Trent and Second Vatican Council

(495) Pope Paul VI

(496) Only two (Catholicism and Orthodox)

(497) Council of Jerusalem

(498) Richard Cardinal Cushing

(499) Theodosius I

(500) General Manuel Noriega

(501) Saint Rose of Lima (1586–1617)

(502) Aztec corn-harvest goddess

(503) Angel of Portugal

(504) 1978 (Pope Paul VI, Pope John Paul I, and Pope John Paul II)

(505) Pope Paul VI (in 1964)

(506) Brooklyn

Chapter 5

(507) Almsgiving

(508) Code of Canon Law

(509) Excommunication

(510) Joyful, Sorrowful, Glorious, and Luminous (Luminous Mysteries are optional)

(511) Sacrilegious

(512) Stigmata

(513) Five of each

(514) False

(515) 1970

(516) (c) 3,000

(517) False

114

(518) Mortal and venial

(519) Forty-six

(520) Dispensation

(521) Good news or good tidings

(522) Books of the Catholic Bible that are non-existent in Protestant versions

(523) Martyr

(524) Adoration

(525) Confraternity of Christian Doctrine

(526) True

(527) Immaculate Conception

(528) True

(529) Holy Spirit

(530) One God, for all eternity

(531) Glorious

(532) *Catechism*

(533) Rubrics

(534) Bright Week

(535) Canon of Sacred Scripture

(536) Apostolic Succession

(537) Apostolate

(538) True

(539) Agnostic

(540) "shall be comforted"

(541) Episcopal

(542) The Annunciation

(543) Put a lighted candle or light in their front window during Advent

(544) Eight (including the pope as Bishop of Rome)

(545) Nine

(546) Parishioner

(547) Pilgrimage

(548) Initiation

(549) Petition

(550) Five Sorrowful Mysteries

(551) Praise the Lord

(552) Amen

(553) Children of God

(554) At least once a year during the Easter season

(555) True

(556) Excommunication

(557) Corporal Works of Mercy

(558) Pope's baptismal name

(559) False

(560) "shall inherit the earth"

(561) Sin

(562) Halos

1981 ▶ Pope John Paul II nearly assassinated by Mehmet Ali Ağca.

(563) Twenty-two

(564) Hope

(565) Automatic excommunication

(566) Paschal Mystery (sometimes called the Passion)

(567) Doctor of the Church

(568) The Beatitudes

(569) Mortification

(570) Uriel

(571) Holy Ghost

(572) One

(573) Parochial school

(574) Capital (also called Deadly)

(575) Mysteries

(576) Idolatry

(577) Discretion to add a fifteenth station, the Resurrection

(578) Phoenix

(579) Evangelization

(580) Votive Mass

(581) Eighteen

(582) Atheism

(583) The Resurrection

(584) Incarnation

(585) Ministry

(586) Laity

(587) Seminary

(588) Purgatory

(589) Ecumenical Council

(590) Agony in the Garden

(591) Charisms

(592) Faith, Hope, and Love (also called Charity)

(593) (1) Epiphany, (2) The Body and Blood of Christ, (3) Saint Joseph, and (4) Saints Peter and Paul

(594) Intentional homicide, abortion, euthanasia, and suicide

(595) Father, Son, and Holy Spirit

(596) Archdiocese

(597) A relic

(598) Miracle

(599) Three elements of mortal sin

(600) Vigil of Easter

(601) Twenty-seven

(602) Water and medicine

(603) Apologetic

(604) Presumption

(605) Brown

(606) Servant of God

(607) Madonna

(608) Annulment

1984 ▶ The first World Youth Day is instituted by Pope John Paul II.

(609) Peter's Pence

(610) Universal

(611) One, Holy, Catholic, and Apostolic

(612) Consistory

(613) Sorrows of Mary

(614) Blessed or happy

(615) Temperance, Fortitude, Prudence, and Justice

(616) Viaticum

(617) Seven (The Seven Great Councils of the Early Church)

(618) Laicization

(619) Blasphemy

(620) Tithe (tithing)

(621) Counselors, Governors, and Messengers

Chapter 6

(622) Chalice

(623) Pentecost, meaning "fiftieth" in Greek

(624) Forehead, lips, and chest (heart)

(625) Ablution

(626) Solemnity

(627) Ash Wednesday

(628) Vigil

(629) Cincture

(630) Easter Sunday

(631) Kyrie Eleison

(632) Font

(633) Every three years

(634) Good Friday

(635) A fish

(636) Peacock

(637) Liturgy of the Eucharist

(638) Holy, Holy, Holy Lord

(639) November

(640) Sacred Heart of Jesus

(641) Pure beeswax

(642) Solemnity of Christ the King

(643) Epiphany

(644) Thurible or censer

(645) Sacristan

(646) Saint Paul and Saint James

(647) "Body of Christ" or "Blood of Christ"

(648) Alb

(649) Immovable feast days

(650) Paschal (or Christ) candle

(651) Holy Days of Obligation

(652) Solemnity of the Annunciation

1985 ▶ **The Lateran Treaty is replaced by a new Vatican-Italy concordat.**

(653) Sunday after Pentecost

(654) Saint Joseph the Worker (May 1st)

(655) Pall

(656) Sign of the cross

(657) Fourteen

(658) Sacring Bell (also known as the Santus Bell)

(659) Ordo

(660) Precious Blood of Our Lord

(661) Litany

(662) Divine Infancy

(663) Lent

(664) Holy water

(665) False (it's discretionary)

(666) Unleavened bread

(667) Concelebrated Mass

(668) Solemnity of the Annunciation

(669) Lent

(670) Gaudete Sunday

(671) Saturday Mass to fulfill the Sunday obligation

(672) Advent and Lent

(673) Credence table

(674) Predella

(675) Symbolizes our desire to spread the "Good News"

(676) 1978

(677) Baldachin or baldachino

(678) Lector

(679) Red (black is sometimes used)

(680) Pentecost

(681) Tabernacle

(682) False (must be ordained)

(683) San Gennaro (Saint Januarius)

(684) Communion Paten

(685) Bow

(686) Violet (often called purple)

(687) Baptistry (or baptistery)

(688) Votive or vigil candles

(689) Mensa

(690) Narthex

(691) Easter Vigil

(692) Holy Rosary

(693) Cruet

(694) Palms from Palm Sunday

(695) Organ

(696) All Saints' Day

(697) Pyx

(698) Green

(699) "Lift up your hearts."

(700) Easter Sunday

ANSWERS

1992 ▶ Vatican officially closes the case against Galileo Galilei in his favor.

(701) Ambry

(702) Three readings instead of two

(703) Tabernacle

(704) Forty-six (Sundays are not counted in the liturgical calendar)

(705) Paten

(706) Spy Wednesday

(707) Cappa Magna

(708) Ciborium

(709) Amphora

(710) Cantor

(711) Three (two readings and the Gospel)

(712) Ascension

(713) Altar

(714) Homily

(715) Recessional

(716) All Saints' Day

(717) 400 years

(718) Liturgy of the Word

(719) True

(720) Intinction

(721) 1977

(722) Queen of Heaven (Latin: Regina Caeli)

(723) Ash Wednesday, dedication of a church building, and consecration of altars

(724) Shrove Tuesday

(725) False (Eucharist means "thanksgiving" while Holy Communion means "union with")

(726) "life everlasting"

(727) One pink and three purple

(728) Pew

(729) Sacristy

(730) Invocation of the Holy Trinity

(731) Missal

(732) Gloria in Excelsis Deo

(733) Our Lady of Guadalupe

(734) January 1st

(735) August

(736) Corporal

(737) Feast of the Holy Family

(738) Nave

(739) Liturgy of the Hours

(740) Antependium

(741) Sacrarium or piscina

(742) "And also with you."

(743) Advent

(744) "Lord, hear our prayer."

(745) "The Mass is ended, go in peace."

(746) Sanctuary

(747) Poinsettia

(748) Liturgy

(749) Typically every twenty-five years

(750) Sanctuary candle

(751) Lilly

(752) Offered for the people with no specific intention

(753) Transubstantiation

(754) Breviary

(755) Epiphany

(756) Purificator

(757) Manuterge

(758) Aspergillum

(759) Choir

(760) Lent

(761) Easter Sunday

(762) A half fish

(763) Holy Week (also called Passion Week)

(764) Immaculate Conception (December 8th)

(765) Solemnity of Saints Peter and Paul

(766) Confessional

(767) Reliquary

(768) Eating of eggs (Easter eggs) on Easter Sunday

(769) Our Father

(770) Aspersory

(771) Prie-dieu

(772) Paschal Triduum (also known as Easter Triduum)

(773) Holy Name of Jesus

(774) Chasuble

(775) Saint Peter and Saint John

(776) Beginning

(777) Olive oil with small amounts of balm

(778) Lavabo

(779) (1) Solemnity, (2) Feast, (3) Memorial (then followed by optional memorial)

Chapter 7

(780) Rosary

(781) Ave Maria

(782) Black

(783) Stations of the Cross

(784) Anointing of the Sick

ANSWERS

2001 ▶ **Forty-four new members of the College of Cardinals are named.**

(785) Bishop

(786) Anointing of the Sick

(787) Sacraments

(788) Blue

(789) Holy Chrism

(790) Sacramentals

(791) Hail Holy Queen

(792) Mortal sin

(793) Rosary

(794) Matrimony and Holy Orders

(795) Absolution

(796) Red

(797) Wisdom

(798) Reconciliation

(799) Holy Hour

(800) Wine, salt, and ashes

(801) Sixteen

(802) Thumb

(803) Holy Chrism

(804) Jesus is Condemned to Death

(805) Fifteen (twenty with optional Luminous Mysteries)

(806) Novena

(807) Holy Orders

(808) 153

(809) Flax or hemp

(810) Age of reason (completion of seventh year)

(811) Dearest

(812) Catechumen

(813) True

(814) Eucharist and Reconciliation

(815) Litany of the Saints

(816) Holy Orders

(817) Litany of the Blessed Sacrament

(818) True

(819) Original sin

(820) Lord's Prayer (also known as the Our Father)

(821) Deacon, priest, and bishop

(822) Apostles' Creed

(823) Confirmation

(824) Confession

(825) Women saints mentioned in the Litany of the Saints

(826) (b) Athanasian Creed

(827) Twelve

(828) Confirmation

(829) Nicene Creed

(830) Memorare

(831) Confiteor

(832) Eucharist

(833) Angelus

(834) Jesus Meets His Sorrowful Mother

(835) Hail Mary

(836) Life

(837) Baptism, Confirmation, and Holy Orders

(838) One

(839) Matrimony

(840) Forehead

(841) Luminous Mysteries

(842) True

(843) Anointing of the Sick

(844) Aspersion (sprinkling), infusion (pouring), and immersion (dipping or plunging)

(845) Anointing of the Sick

(846) Sixteen for males and fourteen for females

(847) Matthew (seven petitions) and Luke (five petitions)

(848) Godparents

(849) *O Come, All Ye Faithful*

(850) Reconciliation and Anointing of the Sick

(851) The Annunciation and Visitation

(852) Three

(853) Invocation

(854) Fifteen

(855) Baptism

(856) A crucifix holds the image of Christ's body, while a cross does not

(857) Baptism, Eucharist, Reconciliation (Penance), Confirmation, Holy Orders (Ordination), Matrimony, and Anointing of the Sick

(858) At least once a year

(859) Instrument of Thy Peace

(860) Act of Contrition

(861) Jesus Takes up His Cross

(862) Fourteen (with an optional new fifteenth)

(863) After childbirth for recovery

(864) Octagon (eight sided)

(865) Reconciliation

(866) Baptism

(867) Six

(868) Chrismation

(869) Intercession

(870) Baptism, Confirmation, and Eucharist

(871) Book of Kells

(872) Apostles' Creed

(873) Monstrance

(874) Matrimony and Holy Orders

(875) Jesus is Taken Down from the Cross

(876) Ten

(877) Holy Orders

(878) Jesus is Placed in the Tomb

(879) False

(880) Holy Orders and Confirmation

(881) Sacramentals

(882) Immersion

(883) White

(884) Dominican Rosary

(885) Hail Holy Queen

(886) Nicene Creed

(887) Hail Mary

Chapter 8

(888) Stole

(889) Knights of Columbus

(890) Mother Angelica

(891) Order of Preachers

(892) Franciscans, Dominicans, Carmelites, Augustinians, and Servites

(893) Mother Teresa

(894) Deacons

(895) Poverty, chastity, and obedience

(896) Permanent diaconate

(897) Habit

(898) Bishops

(899) Rector

(900) Convent

(901) Red

(902) Society of Jesus (Jesuits)

(903) Catholic Relief Services (CRS)

(904) Abbess

(905) Outer vestment worn by deacons

(906) Vicar

(907) Scapular

(908) Cell

(909) Oratory of Saint Philip Neri (Oratorians)

(910) Saint Padre Pio

(911) United States Conference of Catholic Bishops (USCCB)

(912) University of Notre Dame, Saint Mary's College, and Holy Cross College

(913) Auxiliary bishop

(914) Jesuit Order

(915) Ursulines

(916) Diocesan or secular priests

(917) Jesuits use S.J. while Benedictines use O.S.B.

(918) Surplice

(919) Catholic Theological Society

(920) Seventy-five

(921) Diocese

(922) Third finger of the right hand

(923) Mother Pasqualina Lehnert

(924) Friars and monks

(925) Zucchetto

(926) Catholic Answers

(927) Thirty-five

(928) Salesians of Don Bosco

(929) New York (South Bronx)

(930) Contemplative prayer

(931) Father Damien de Veuster (1840–1889)

(932) Archbishop Fulton J. Sheen (1895–1979)

(933) **C**atholic **Y**outh **O**rganization

(934) Catechist

(935) Nun

(936) Bishops

(937) Cardinals

(938) Catholic League for Religious and Civil Rights

(939) Bishops, archbishops, and patriarchs

(940) *The Liguorian*

(941) Fr. Gabriel Richard

(942) Vows of poverty, chastity, and obedience

(943) Novice

(944) **R**ite of **C**hristian **I**nitiation of **A**dults

(945) Superior or superior general

(946) Jesuit Order

(947) *America*

(948) Refectory

(949) Order of the Brothers of Our Lady of Mount Carmel (Carmelites)

(950) 1979

(951) Cowl

(952) Zimmarra

(953) Pallium

(954) India

(955) Rectory

(956) Bishops

(957) True

(958) Paris, France

CHAPTER 9

ANSWERS

2008 ▶ Pope Benedict XVI participates in Sydney for the World Youth Day.

(959) Forty-three percent

(960) Bishop

(961) Dominican Order

(962) Beg (from Bègue, the founder)

(963) Coadjutor bishop

(964) Miter (or Mitre)

(965) Celibacy

(966) True

(967) (b) Irish

(968) Dom Pérignon (c.1638–1715)

(969) Servant (may also mean minister or messenger)

(970) Basilians

(971) Maryknoll

(972) *St. Anthony Messenger*

(973) Benedictine (Bleu Bénédictin)

(974) Augustinians

(975) Three

(976) Crosier (or crozier)

(977) Monsignor

(978) Father Edward Flanagan (1886–1948)

(979) 41,406

(980) Pectoral cross

(981) Saint Dominic de Guzmán

(982) Catholic World News

(983) Paulist

(984) Saints Clare of Assisi and Francis of Assisi, in 1212

(985) Permanent diaconate

(986) True

(987) Fourteen Holy Helpers

(988) DePaul University

(989) Chaplain

(990) Nun and sister

(991) Cassock

(992) Buried with them

(993) Carmelite Order

(994) Passionist

(995) Sisters of Mercy

(996) Coif

(997) Anglican

(998) Eternal Word Television Network (EWTN)

(999) Popes

(1000) (d) 1882

(1001) Priests who served in the United States Congress

No.	Pontiff	Pontificate From	To
1	St. Peter	32	67
2	St. Linus	67	76
3	St. Anacletus (Cletus)	76	88
4	St. Clement I	88	97
5	St. Evaristus	97	105
6	St. Alexander I	105	115
7	St. Sixtus I	115	125
8	St. Telesphorus	125	136
9	St. Hyginus	136	140
10	St. Pius I	140	155
11	St. Anicetus	155	166
12	St. Soter	166	175
13	St. Eleutherius	175	189
14	St. Victor I	189	199
15	St. Zephyrinus	199	217
16	St. Callistus I	217	222
17	St. Urban I	222	230
18	St. Pontain	230	235
19	St. Anterus	235	236
20	St. Fabian	236	250
21	St. Cornelius	251	253
22	St. Lucius I	253	254
23	St. Stephen I	254	257
24	St. Sixtus II	257	258
25	St. Dionysius	260	268
26	St. Felix I	269	274
27	St. Eutychian	275	283
28	St. Caius (Gaius)	283	296
29	St. Marcellinus	296	304
30	St. Marcellus I	308	309
31	St. Eusebius	309	310
32	St. Miltiades	311	314
33	St. Sylvester I	314	335
34	St. Marcus	336	336
35	St. Julius I	337	352

No.	Pontiff	Pontificate From	To
36	Liberius	352	366
37	St. Damasus I	366	383
38	St. Siricius	384	399
39	St. Anastasius I	399	401
40	St. Innocent I	401	417
41	St. Zosimus	417	418
42	St. Boniface I	418	422
43	St. Celestine I	422	432
44	St. Sixtus III	432	440
45	St. Leo I (the Great)	440	461
46	St. Hilarius (Hilarus)	461	468
47	St. Simplicius	468	483
48	St. Felix III (II)	483	492
49	St. Gelasius I	492	496
50	St. Anastasius II	496	498
51	St. Symmachus	498	514
52	St. Hormisdas	514	523
53	St. John I	523	526
54	St. Felix IV (III)	526	530
55	Boniface II	530	532
56	John II	533	535
57	St. Agapitus I (Agapetus)	535	536
58	St. Silverius	536	537
59	Vigilius	537	555
60	Pelagius I	556	561
61	John III	561	574
62	Benedict I	575	579
63	Pelagius II	579	590
64	St. Gregory (the Great)	590	604
65	Sabinian	604	606
66	Boniface III	607	607
67	St. Boniface IV	608	615
68	St. Deusdedit (Adeodatus I)	615	618
69	Boniface V	619	625
70	Honorius I	625	638

No.	Pontiff	Pontificate From	Pontificate To
71	Severinus	640	640
72	John IV	640	642
73	Theodore I	642	649
74	St. Martin I	649	655
75	St. Eugene I	655	657
76	St. Vitalian	657	672
77	Adeodatus II	672	676
78	Donus	676	678
79	St. Agatho	678	681
80	St. Leo II	682	683
81	St. Benedict II	684	685
82	John V	685	686
83	Conon	686	687
84	St. Sergius I	687	701
85	John VI	701	705
86	John VII	705	707
87	Sisinnius	708	708
88	Constantine	708	715
89	St. Gregory II	715	731
90	St. Gregory III	731	741
91	St. Zachary	741	752
92	Stephen II	752	752
93	St. Paul I	757	767
94	Stephen III	767	772
95	Adrian I (Hadrian)	772	795
96	St. Leo III	795	816
97	Stephen IV	816	817
98	St. Paschal I	817	824
99	Eugene II	824	827
100	Valentine	827	827
101	Gregory IV	827	844
102	Sergius II	844	847
103	St. Leo IV	847	855
104	Benedict III	855	858
105	St. Nicholas I (the Great)	858	867
106	Adrian II (Hadrian)	867	872
107	John VIII	872	882
108	Marinus I	882	884
109	St. Adrian III (Hadrian)	884	885
110	Stephen V	885	891

No.	Pontiff	Pontificate From	Pontificate To
111	Formosus	891	896
112	Boniface VI	896	896
113	Stephen VI	896	897
114	Romanus	897	897
115	Theodore II	897	897
116	John IX	898	900
117	Benedict IV	900	903
118	Leo V	903	903
119	Sergius III	904	911
120	Anastasius III	911	913
121	Lando (Landus)	913	914
122	John X	914	928
123	Leo VI	928	928
124	Stephen VII	929	931
125	John XI	931	935
126	Leo VII	936	939
127	Stephen VIII	939	942
128	Marinus II	942	946
129	Agapetus II (Agapitus)	946	955
130	John XII	955	963
131	Leo VIII	963	964
132	Benedict V	964	964
133	John XIII	965	972
134	Benedict VI	973	974
135	Benedict VII	974	983
136	John XIV	983	984
137	John XV	985	996
138	Gregory V	996	999
139	Sylvester II	999	1003
140	John XVII	1003	1003
141	John XVIII	1003	1009
142	Sergius IV	1009	1012
143	Benedict VIII	1012	1024
144	John XIX	1024	1032
145	Benedict IX	1032	1045
146	Sylvester III	1045	1045
147	Benedict IX	1045	1045
148	Gregory VI	1045	1046
149	Clement II	1046	1047
150	Benedict IX	1047	1048

No.	Pontiff	Pontificate From	Pontificate To
151	Damasus II	1048	1048
152	St. Leo IX	1049	1054
153	Victor II	1055	1057
154	Stephen IX	1057	1058
155	Nicholas II	1058	1061
156	Alexander II	1061	1073
157	St. Gregory VII	1073	1085
158	Blessed Victor III	1086	1087
159	Blessed Urban II	1088	1099
160	Paschal II	1099	1118
161	Gelasius II	1118	1119
162	Callistus II	1119	1124
163	Honorius II	1124	1130
164	Innocent II	1130	1143
165	Celestine II	1143	1144
166	Lucius II	1144	1145
167	Blessed Eugene III	1145	1153
168	Anastasius IV	1153	1154
169	Adrian IV (Hadrian)	1154	1159
170	Alexander III	1159	1181
171	Lucius III	1181	1185
172	Urban III	1185	1187
173	Gregory VIII	1187	1187
174	Clement III	1187	1191
175	Celestine III	1191	1198
176	Innocent III	1198	1216
177	Honorius III	1216	1227
178	Gregory IX	1227	1241
179	Celestine IV	1241	1241
180	Innocent IV	1243	1254
181	Alexander IV	1254	1261
182	Urban IV	1261	1264
183	Clement IV	1265	1268
184	Blessed Gregory X	1271	1276
185	Blessed Innocent V	1276	1276
186	Adrian V (Hadrian)	1276	1276
187	John XXI	1276	1277
188	Nicholas III	1277	1280
189	Martin IV	1281	1285
190	Honorius IV	1285	1287

No.	Pontiff	Pontificate From	Pontificate To
191	Nicholas IV	1288	1292
192	St. Celestine V	1294	1294
193	Boniface VIII	1294	1303
194	Blessed Benedict XI	1303	1304
195	Clement V	1305	1314
196	John XXII	1316	1334
197	Benedict XII	1334	1342
198	Clement VI	1342	1352
199	Innocent VI	1352	1362
200	Blessed Urban V	1362	1370
201	Gregory XI	1370	1378
202	Urban VI	1378	1389
203	Boniface IX	1389	1404
204	Innocent VII	1406	1406
205	Gregory XII	1406	1415
206	Martin V	1417	1431
207	Eugene IV	1431	1447
208	Nicholas V	1447	1455
209	Callistus III	1445	1458
210	Pius II	1458	1464
211	Paul II	1464	1471
212	Sixtus IV	1471	1484
213	Innocent VIII	1484	1492
214	Alexander VI	1492	1503
215	Pius III	1503	1503
216	Julius II	1503	1513
217	Leo X	1513	1521
218	Adrian VI (Hadrian)	1522	1523
219	Clement VII	1523	1534
220	Paul III	1534	1549
221	Julius III	1550	1555
222	Marcellus II	1555	1555
223	Paul IV	1555	1559
224	Pius IV	1559	1565
225	St. Pius V	1566	1572
226	Gregory XIII	1572	1585
227	Sixtus V	1585	1590
228	Urban VII	1590	1590
229	Gregory XIV	1590	1591
230	Innocent IX	1591	1591

No.	Pontiff	Pontificate	
		From	To
231	Clement VIII	1592	1605
232	Leo XI	1605	1605
233	Paul V	1605	1621
234	Gregory XV	1621	1623
235	Urban VIII	1623	1644
236	Innocent X	1644	1655
237	Alexander VII	1655	1667
238	Clement IX	1667	1669
239	Clement X	1670	1676
240	Blessed Innocent XI	1676	1689
241	Alexander VIII	1689	1691
242	Innocent XII	1691	1700
243	Clement XI	1700	1721
244	Innocent XIII	1721	1724
245	Benedict XIII	1724	1730
246	Clement XII	1730	1740
247	Benedict XIV	1740	1758
248	Clement XIII	1758	1769
249	Clement XIV	1769	1774
250	Pius VI	1775	1799
251	Pius VII	1800	1823
252	Leo XII	1823	1829
253	Pius VIII	1829	1830
254	Gregory XVI	1831	1846
255	Ven. Pius IX	1846	1878
256	Leo XIII	1878	1903
257	St. Pius X	1903	1914
258	Benedict XV	1914	1922
259	Pius XI	1922	1939
260	Pius XII	1939	1958
261	Blessed John XXIII	1958	1963
262	Paul VI	1963	1978
263	John Paul I	1978	1978
264	John Paul II	1978	2005
265	Benedict XVI	2005	

APPENDIX B: MAP OF VATICAN CITY

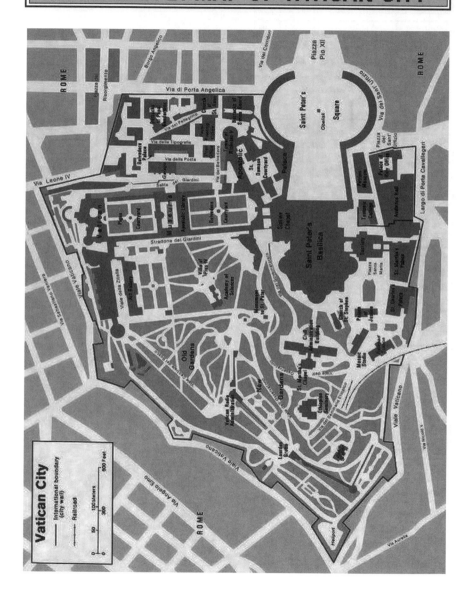

BIBLIOGRAPHY

❖ BUNSON, MATTHEW, *2009 Catholic Almanac*, Huntington, Indiana: Our Sunday Visitor, 2009

❖ BUNSON, MATTHEW, *Encyclopedia of Catholic History*, Huntington, Indiana: Our Sunday Visitor, 2004

❖ BUNSON, MATTHEW; BUNSON, MARGARET; & BUNSON, STEPHEN, *Encyclopedia of Saints*, Huntington, Indiana: Our Sunday Visitor, 2003

❖ CUNNINGHAM, LAWRENCE S., *The Catholic Faith: An Introduction*, Mahwah, New Jersey: Paulist Press, 1986

❖ DUBRUIEL, MICHAEL, *The How-To Book of the Mass*, Huntington, Indiana: Our Sunday Visitor, 2002

❖ FOLEY, MICHAEL, *Why Do Catholics Eat Fish on Friday?*, New York: Palgrave Macmillan, 2005

❖ JOHNSON, KEVIN ORLIN, *Why Do Catholics Do That?*, New York: Ballantine Books, 1994

❖ KLEIN, PETER REV., *The Catholic Sourcebook*, Orlando, Florida: Harcourt Religion Publishers, 2000

❖ KNOWLES, LEO, *Catholic Book of Quotations*, Huntington, Indiana: Our Sunday Visitor, 2004

❖ LO BELLO, NINO, *The Incredible Book of Vatican Facts and Papal Curiosities*, New York: Barnes & Noble Books, 1998

❖ STRAVINSKAS, PETER, M.J., *Catholic Encyclopedia*, Huntington, Indiana: Our Sunday Visitor, 1998

❖ TRIGILIO, JOHN REV. & BRIGHENTI, KENNETH REV., *Catholicism for Dummies*, New York: Wiley Publishing, 2003

❖ UNITED STATES CONFERENCE OF CATHOLIC BISHOPS, *United States Catholic Catechism for Adults*, Washington, D.C.: USCCB Publishing, 2006

❖ WRIGHT, KEVIN J., *Catholic Shrines of Western Europe: A Pilgrim's Travel Guide*, Liguori, Missouri: Liguori Publications, 1997

ORDER FORM

Telephone Orders: (800) 431-1579

Internet Orders: www.Amazon.com

Fax Orders: (248) 232-1501 (credit card only – please include this form)

Postal Orders: Marshall Rand Publishing
P.O. Box 1849
Royal Oak, MI 48068-1849

Postal orders receive author signed copies

▶ Make check payable to *Marshall Rand Publishing*

Ship to:

Name:_____

Address:_____

City:_____ State:_____ Zip:_____

Telephone:_____

Item:

Book: ***Ultimate Catholic Trivia***   ($9.95 each) $ _____
1001 Fun and Fascinating Facts

Postage: ($2.50 first book, $0.50 each additional book) $_____

Sales Tax: (Michigan residents, add $0.60 for each book) $ _____

Total: (please sum all amounts) $_____

Payment: ☐ Check   ☐ Visa   ☐ MasterCard

Card number:_____

Name on card:_____ Exp. Date:_____